> One-Minute Devotions

Family Blessings on which to Build

Dr. JAMES DOBSON

CHRISTIAN ART
Vereeniging

Material in this book is adapted from *FAMILY BUILDERS* calendar with permission from Tyndale House Publishers. © 1993 by James Dobson Inc.

Quotations from the following books of James Dobson. From FOCUS ON THE FAMILY: ***Values in the Home*** (booklet), 1990. From MULTNOMAH: ***Love for a Lifetime***, 1987. From REGAL: ***Emotions: Can You Trust Them?*** 1980. From REVELL: ***Hide or Seek***, 1974, 1979. From TYNDALE HOUSE: ***Dare to Discipline***, 1970; ***Dr. Dobson Answers Your Questions***, 1982; *T**he New Dare to Discipline***, 1992; ***The Strong-Willed Child***, 1978; ***What Wives Wish Their Husbands Knew about Women***, 1975. From WORD INC., Dallas, Texas: ***Children at Risk***, 1990; ***Love Must Be Tough***, 1983; ***Parenting Isn't for Cowards***, 1987; ***Straight Talk to Men and Their Wives***, 1980, 1984. Scripture verses marked TLB are from ***The Living Bible***, copyright © 1971 owned by assignment by KNT Charitable Trust. All rights reserved. Scripture verses marked NIV are from the ***Holy Bible***, New International Version. Copyright © 1973, 1978, 1984 International Bible Society. Used by permission of Zondervan Bible Publishers. Scripture verses marked KJV are from the King James Version of the Bible.

FAMILY BLESSINGS ON WHICH TO BUILD

© 1995 Christian Art, P.O. Box 1599, Vereeniging, South Africa.

ISBN 1-86852-056-0

All rights reserved.

Printed in Singapore.

JANUARY

JANUARY 1

CONSTANT SATISFACTION

Satisfy us in the morning with your unfailing love, that we may sing for joy and be glad all our days.
Psalm 90:14 NIV

Children of all ages seek constant satisfaction of their emotional needs, including the desire for love, social acceptance, and self-respect.

JANUARY 2

GODLINESS

Godliness exalts a nation.
Proverbs 14:34 TLB

When a nation is composed of millions of devoted, responsible family units, the entire society is stable, responsible, and resilient.

JANUARY 3

THE HOPE OF THE FUTURE

"For I know the plans I have for you," declares the LORD, "plans to prosper you and not to harm you, plans to give you hope and a future."
Jeremiah 29:11 NIV

Children, yours and mine, are the true wealth of any nation, and in them lies the hope of the future. A society that is too busy or too preoccupied for its children is just a nation of aging, dying people who feed on their own selfish interests.

JANUARY 4

THE TASK OF PARENTING

If any of you lack wisdom, let him ask of God, that giveth to all men liberally, and upbraideth not; and it shall be given him.
James 1:5 KJV

The task of parenting is too scary on our own, and there is not enough knowledge on the books to guarantee the outcome of our parenting duties. We desperately need divine help with the job!

JANUARY 5

CHILDREN OF GOD!

*How great is the love the Father
has lavished on us, that we
should be called children of God!*
1 John 3:1 NIV

When a child is convinced he is greatly loved and respected by his parents, he is inclined to accept his own worth as a person.

JANUARY 6

THE RECORD

All that is now hidden will someday come to light.
Mark 4:22 TLB

When the story of your family is finally written, what will the record show?

JANUARY 7

THE PARENTAL ASSIGNMENT

I can do everything through him who gives me strength.
Philippians 4:13 NIV

Raising kids properly is one of life's richest challenges. It is not uncommon to feel overwhelmed by the complexity of the parental assignment.

JANUARY 8

FAMILY IS IMPORTANT

*Keep on sowing your seed,
for you never know which will
grow – perhaps it all will.*
Ecclesiastes 11:6 TLB

Do you show your child that you feel your family is important by spending time together, loving one another, supporting one another?

JANUARY 9

WELL-ROOTED

They will be called oaks of righteousness, a planting of the LORD, for the display of his splendor.
Isaiah 61:3 NIV

A mesquite tree planted in a desert is threatened by its hostile environment. It survives by sending its roots deep into the earth, and so, the well-rooted tree becomes strong and steady against all assailants. In the same way children who have learned to conquer their problems are more secure than those who have never faced them.

JANUARY 10

OBEDIENCE TO GOD?

To do what is right and just is more acceptable to the Lord than sacrifice.
Proverbs 21:3 NIV

Is your child learning to obey you as preparation for later obedience to God?

JANUARY 11

CONSISTENT INFLUENCE

Praise the LORD, O my soul, and forget not all his benefits – who forgives all your sins and heals all your diseases, who redeems your life from the pit and crowns you with love and compassion.
Psalm 103:2-4 NIV

Fortunately, we are permitted to make a few mistakes with our children. It is not the few errors that destroy a child. It is the consistent influence of conditions throughout childhood.

JANUARY 12

SUBMIT TO THE FATHER

We have all had human fathers who disciplined us ... How much more should we submit to the Father of our spirits and live!
Hebrews 12:9 NIV

Virtually all of our founding fathers revered the Lord and looked to him for strength and wisdom. Today we cling to the same source of confidence and hope. Yes, our families are pitching and rolling like ships on a stormy sea. But we believe they can be sailed again into the safe harbor of peace and harmony.

JANUARY 13

MATERIALISM

*For the love of money is
the root of all evil.*
1 Timothy 6:10 KJV

The love of money is the root of all evil. That's why Jesus issues more warnings about materialism and wealth than any other sin.

JANUARY 14

A CHILD'S ACCEPTANCE

For God said, "Honor your father and mother."
Matthew 15:4 NIV

A child's attitude toward his parents' leadership is critical to his acceptance of their values and philosophy.

JANUARY 15

CONFORMITY

Do not love the world or anything in the world ... The world and its desires pass away, but the man who does the will of God lives forever.
1 John 2:15, 17 NIV

Children are very concerned about the threat of being laughed at by their friends and will sometimes go to great lengths to avoid that possibility. Conformity is fueled by the fear of ridicule. Teens, particularly, seem to feel, "The group can't laugh at me if I am identical to them."

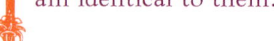

JANUARY 16

GUARD MY TEACHINGS

My son, keep my words and store up my commands within you. Keep my commands and you will live; guard my teachings as the apple of your eye.
Proverbs 7:1-2 NIV

In the matter of sex education, the best approach begins in early childhood and extends through the years, according to a policy of openness, frankness, and honesty. Only parents can provide this lifetime training.

JANUARY 17

EVERY MOMENT

Be wise: make the most of every opportunity you have for doing good.
Ephesians 5:15-16 TLB

Our sons and daughters will be grown so quickly and these days at home together will be nothing but a distant memory. Let's make the most of every moment.

JANUARY 18

SOMETHING OF GREAT WORTH

A wise woman builds her house, while a foolish woman tears hers down by her own efforts.
Proverbs 14:1 TLB

Where does your marriage rank on your hierarchy of values? Does it get the leftovers and scraps from your busy schedule, or is it something of great worth to be preserved and supported? It can die if left untended.

JANUARY 19

THE INSIGNIFICANCE OF MATERIALISM

Your riches won't help you on Judgment Day; only righteousness counts then ... Trust in your money and down you go! Trust in God and flourish as a tree!
Proverbs 11:4, 28 TLB

Is your child learning the relative insignificance of materialism?

JANUARY 20

TRUE VALUES

These are the commands, decrees and laws the LORD your God directed me to teach you to observe ... so that you, your children and their children after them may fear the Lord your God as long as you live by keeping all his decrees and commands that I give you, and so that you may enjoy life.
Deuteronomy 6:1-2 NIV

Begin very early to instruct your child on the true values of life: love, kindness, integrity, trustworthiness, devotion to God, etc. Herein lies the anchor that can hold a child steady.

JANUARY 21

READING THE BIBLE

*Those who love your laws
have great peace of heart
and mind and do not stumble.*
Psalm 119:165 TLB

Is your child learning to read the Bible?

JANUARY 22

THE BEGINNING OF WISDOM

The fear of the LORD is the beginning of wisdom, and knowledge of the Holy One is understanding.
Proverbs 9:10 NIV

There is a brief period during childhood when youngsters are vulnerable to religious training. Their concepts of right and wrong are formulated during this time, and their view of God begins to solidify.

JANUARY 23

GOD'S MIGHTY WEAPONS

I use God's mighty weapons ... to knock down the devil's strongholds ... With these weapons I can capture rebels and bring them back to God.
2 Corinthians 10:4-5 TLB

The strong-willed adolescent simply must not be given large quantities of unstructured time. He will find destructive ways to use such moments. Get him involved in the very best church youth program and other activities you can find.

JANUARY 24

NUMBER YOUR DAYS

Teach us to number our days and recognize how few they are; help us to spend them as we should.
Psalm 90:12 TLB

Three questions should be asked about every new activity that presents itself: (1) Is it worthy of our time? (2) What will be eliminated if it is added? (3) What will be its impact on our family life?

JANUARY 25

IT TAKES TIME

The Lord ... lets me rest in the meadow grass and leads me beside the quiet streams. He gives me new strength. He helps me do what honors him the most.
Psalm 23:1-3 TLB

Children just don't fit into a "to do" list very well. It takes time to be an effective parent when children are small. It takes time to introduce them to good books – it takes time to fly kites and play punch ball and put together jigsaw puzzles. It takes time to listen.

JANUARY 26

THE FUTURE YOU SHARE

I pray that your hearts will be flooded with light so that you can see something of the future he has called you to share.
Ephesians 1:18 TLB

Marital problems are almost inevitable when couples overcommit themselves during the early years. The bonding that should occur in the first decade requires time together — time that cannot be given if it is absorbed elsewhere. Success will wait, but a happy family will not.

JANUARY 27

PERSEVERANCE

*Let us run with perseverance
the race marked out for us.
Let us fix our eyes on Jesus.*
Hebrews 12:1-2 NIV

Married life is a marathon. It is not enough to make a great start toward long-term marriage. You will need the determination to keep plugging. Only then will you make it to the end. But hang in there.

JANUARY 28

THE MEANING OF SIN

Direct my footsteps according to your word; let no sin rule over me.
Psalm 119:133 NIV

Is your child learning the meaning of sin and its inevitable consequences?

JANUARY 29

CLOSENESS BETWEEN GENERATIONS

If a widow has children or grandchildren, these should learn first of all to put their religion into practice by caring for their own family and so repaying their parents and grandparents, for this is pleasing to God.
1 Timothy 5:4 NIV

Closeness between generations comes from the child's knowledge that his parent understands and appreciates his feelings.

JANUARY 30

A CHILD'S WILL

[A Father] must manage his own family well and see that his children obey him with proper respect.
1 Timothy 3:4-5 NIV

A child's will is a powerful force in the human personality. It is one of the few intellectual components which arrives full strength at the moment of birth. The will is not delicate and wobbly.

JANUARY 31

GOD OF JUSTICE

The LORD longs to be gracious to you; he rises to show you compassion, For the LORD is a God of justice. Blessed are all who wait for him!
Isaiah 30:18 NIV

We should make it clear that the merciful God of love whom we serve is also a God of justice. An adolescent who understands this truth is more likely to live a moral life in the midst of an immoral society.

FEBRUARY

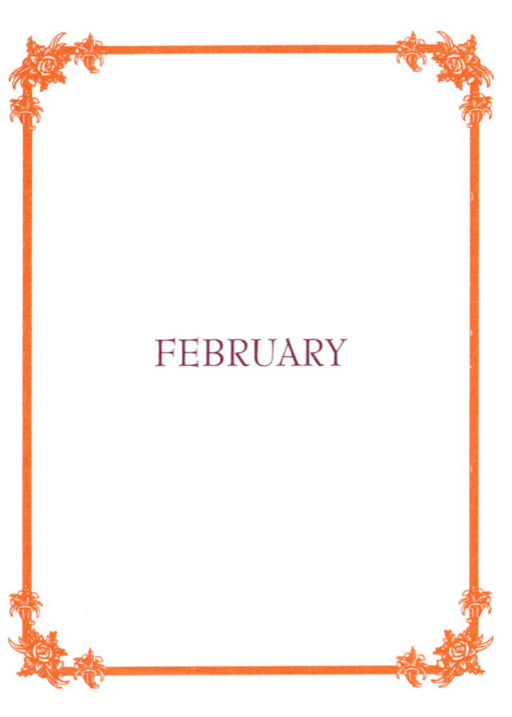

FEBRUARY 1

THE SPIRIT OF A CHILD

The wise in heart are called discerning, and pleasant words promote instruction.
Proverbs 16:21 NIV

The spirit of a child is a million times more vulnerable than his will. It is a delicate flower that can be crushed and broken all too easily (and even unintentionally).

FEBRUARY 2

THE LORD'S PURPOSE

Many are the plans in a man's heart, but it is the LORD'S purpose that prevails.
Proverbs 19:21 NIV

Is your child learning to talk about the Lord, and to include him in his thoughts and plans?

FEBRUARY 3

TEACH THEM

May God be with you. You must be the people's representative before God ... Teach them the decrees and laws, and show them the way to live.
Exodus 18:19-20 NIV

Provide your children with many interesting books and materials, read to them and answer their questions.

FEBRUARY 4

OBEDIENT TO HIM

If we stay close to him, obedient to him, we won't be sinning.
1 John 3:6 TLB

A family builder value: God is like a Father to his children. He loves them more than they can understand, but he also expects them to be obedient to his will.

FEBRUARY 5

REWARD

A word aptly spoken is like apples of gold in settings of silver.
Proverbs 25:11 NIV

Verbal reinforcement should permeate the entire relationship between parent and child. Too often our parental instruction consists of a million "don'ts." We should spend more time rewarding him for the behavior we desire, even if our "reward" is nothing more than a sincere compliment.

FEBRUARY 6

TURN TO JESUS

I will not abandon you or leave you as orphans in the storm – I will come to you.
John 14:18 TLB

Is your child learning to turn to Jesus for help whenever he is frightened or anxious or lonely?

FEBRUARY 7

GIVE AWAY AND BECOME RICHER

It is possible to give away and become richer! It is also possible to hold on too tightly and lose everything.
Proverbs 11:24-25 TLB

Students can't learn without facing some hardships. And ultimately, an adolescent can't enter young adulthood until we release him from our protective custody.

FEBRUARY 8

THE STORMS OF ADOLESCENCE

Let everyone bless God and sing his praises; for he holds our lives in his hands, and he holds our feet to the path.
Psalm 66:8-9 TLB

Don't panic during the storms of adolescence. Better times are ahead.

FEBRUARY 9

CANCERS THAT GNAW

Satan has asked to have you, to sift you like wheat, but I have pleaded in prayer for you.
Luke 22:31 TLB

Infidelity and marital conflict are cancers that gnaw on the soul of mankind, twisting and warping innocent family members who can only stand and watch.

FEBRUARY 10

SCREEN THE INFLUENCES

Do not withhold your mercy from me, O LORD; may your love and your truth always protect me. For troubles without number surround me.
Psalm 40:11-12 NIV

It is desirable to postpone the adolescent experience until it is summoned by the hormones. Therefore, I strongly recommend that parents screen the influences to which their children will be exposed, keeping activities appropriate for each age.

FEBRUARY 11

HIS IMPRINT

Lead them by your good example.
1 Peter 5:3 TLB

A good father will leave his imprint on his children for the rest of their lives.

FEBRUARY 12

SUFFER LITTLE CHILDREN

But Jesus called them unto him, and said, Suffer little children to come unto me, and forbid them not: for of such is the kingdom of God.
Luke 18:16 KJV

Every child is of equal worth in the sight of God.

FEBRUARY 13

AS THEY ARE

Few of you who follow Christ have big names or power or wealth ... so that no one anywhere can ever brag in the presence of God.
1 Corinthians 1:26, 29 TLB

The vast majority of our children are not dazzlingly brilliant, extremely witty, highly coordinated, tremendously talented, or universally popular! They are just plain kids with oversized needs to be loved and accepted as they are.

FEBRUARY 14

CHARACTERIZED BY LOVE

Because of the Lord's great love we are not consumed, for his compassions never fail. They are new every morning; great is your faithfulness.
Lamentations 3:22-23 NIV

The parent's relationship with his child should be modeled after God's relationship with man. In its ultimate beauty, that interaction is characterized by abundant love – a love unparalleled in tenderness and mercy.

FEBRUARY 15

A PERSONAL SACRIFICE

The father of a righteous man has great joy; he who has a wise son delights in him.
Proverbs 23:24 NIV

Being a mother or father is not only one of life's greatest joys, but it can also represent a personal sacrifice and challenge. Everything of value is expensive, and children are no exception to the rule.

FEBRUARY 16

HE KNOWS WHAT IS BEST FOR US

He has showered down upon us the richness of his grace – for how well he understands us and knows what is best for us.
Ephesians 1:8 TLB

Are you secretly disappointed because your child is so ordinary? Was he born during a difficult time for the family? Did you want a girl instead of a boy? Does he embarrass you by being either too loud and rambunctious or too inward and withdrawn?

FEBRUARY 17

THE REWARDS

Everything comes from God alone. Everything lives by his power, and everything is for his glory.
Romans 11:36 TLB

Kids can frustrate and irritate their parents ... but the rewards of raising them far outweigh the cost. Besides, nothing worth having ever comes cheap.

FEBRUARY 18

ULTIMATE LOYALTY

They will be my people, and I will be their God. I will give them singleness of heart and action, so that they will always fear me for their own good and the good of their children after them.
Jeremiah 32:38-39 NIV

Children should also be taught ultimate loyalty to God.

FEBRUARY 19

A FREE CHOICE

I love those who love me, and those who seek me find me.
Proverbs 8:17 NIV

God gave us a free choice because there is no significance to love that knows no alternative.

FEBRUARY 20

A CHEERFUL GIVER

Each man should give what he has decided in his heart to give, not reluctantly or under compulsion, for God loves a cheerful giver.
2 Corinthians 9:7 NIV

God is entitled to a portion of our income. Not because he needs it, but because we need to give it.

FEBRUARY 21

HOPE FOR YOU YET!

You have a wonderful future ahead of you. There is hope for you yet!
Proverbs 23:17-18 TLB

Adolescence is a fascinating and crazy time of life.

FEBRUARY 22

LOVE IS FRAGILE

A woman who fears the LORD is to be praised. Give her the reward she has earned.
Proverbs 31:30-31 NIV

Love, even genuine love, is a fragile thing. It must be maintained and protected if it is to survive. Love can perish when a husband works seven days a week ... when there is no time for romantic activity.

FEBRUARY 23

VIOLENCE IS A REALITY

Let everyone call urgently on God. Let them give up their evil ways and their violence.
Jonah 3:8 NIV

No longer is extreme violence something that happens only on television. It is a reality of daily life for many of our youth.

FEBRUARY 24

DON'T JUST PRETEND

Don't just pretend to be good!
1 Peter 2:1 TLB

Someone has said: We are not what we think we are. We are not even what others think we are. We are what we think others think we are.

FEBRUARY 25

LEARNING TO GIVE

This poor widow has put more into the treasury than all the others. They all gave out of their wealth; but she, out of her poverty, put in everything – all she had to live on.
Mark 12:43-44 NIV

Is your child learning to give a portion of his allowance (and other money) to God?

FEBRUARY 26

ENCOURAGE ONE ANOTHER

Let us consider how we may spur one another on toward love and good deeds ... Let us encourage one another.
Hebrews 10:24-25 NIV

Flattery occurs when you heap compliments upon a child for something he does not achieve, such as his or her beauty or clothing. Praise, on the other hand, is used to reinforce positive, constructive behaviour.

FEBRUARY 27

KIND WORDS

*Kind words are like honey -
enjoyable and healthful.*
Proverbs 16:24 TLB

The most healthy families are those that can laugh together, and I certainly don't think our egos should be so fragile that we all have to walk on cracked eggs around each other. However, even innocent humor can be painful when one child is always the object of ridicule.

FEBRUARY 28

PROPER VALUES

I will rejoice if you become a man of common sense. Yes, my heart will thrill to your thoughtful, wise words.
Proverbs 23:15-16 TLB

We are given 18 or 20 years to interject the proper values and attitudes in our children; then we must take our hands off and trust in divine leadership to influence the outcome.

MARCH

MARCH 1

LOVE MAY ABOUND IN KNOWLEDGE

This is my prayer: that your love may abound more and more in knowledge and depth of insight.
Philippians 1:9 NIV

If we only realized how brief is our time on this earth, then most of the irritants and frustrations that drive us apart would seem terribly insignificant and petty.

MARCH 2

FACE IT WITH COURAGE

"Be strong and courageous. Do not be terrified; do not be discouraged, for the LORD your God will be with you wherever you go."
Joshua 1:9 NIV

Adolescence is not an easy time of life for either generation; in fact, it can be downright terrifying. But the key to surviving this emotional experience is to lay the proper foundation and then face it with courage.

MARCH 3

BELIEVE AND ACCEPT

Be sure to fear the Lord and serve him faithfully with all your heart; consider what great things he has done for you.
1 Samuel 12:24 NIV

The obvious hope is that the adolescent will respect and appreciate his parents enough to believe what they say and accept what they recommend.

MARCH 4

JUDGE NOTHING

Judge nothing before the appointed time; wait till the Lord comes. He will bring to light what is hidden in darkness and will expose the motives of men's hearts. At that time each will receive his praise from God.
1 Corinthians 4:5 NIV

Parents today are much too willing to blame themselves for everything their children or adolescents do.

MARCH 5

A PATIENT MAN

*Better a patient man than a warrior,
a man who controls his temper
than one who takes a city.*
Proverbs 16:32 NIV

Does your child see you practice self-control? For example, do you try to keep your temper in frustrating circumstances?

MARCH 6

LOVE THE LORD THY GOD

Thou shalt love the Lord thy God with all thy heart, and with all thy soul, and with all thy mind, and with all thy strength.
Mark 12:30

Is your child learning of the love of God through your love, tenderness and mercy?

MARCH 7

PRAY FOR ONE ANOTHER

Pray for one another ... The effectual fervent prayer of a righteous man availeth much.
James 5:16 KJV

The Scriptures teach that we can pray effectively for one another and that such a petition "availeth much." I believe God honors and answers this kind of intercessory prayer.

MARCH 8

MORALITY

Blessed are they whose ways are blameless, who walk according to the law of the LORD.
Psalm 119:1 NIV

Because mothers and fathers represent "God" to their children, the fundamental element in teaching morality can be achieved through a healthy parental relationship during the early years.

MARCH 9

TRYING TO UNDERSTAND

For we are God's workmanship, created in Christ Jesus to do good works.
Ephesians 2:10 NIV

Does your child see and hear you trying to understand how other people feel – putting yourself in their shoes?

MARCH 10

FULNESS OF JOY

Thou wilt show me the path of life: in thy presence is fulness of joy; at thy right hand there are pleasures for evermore.
Psalm 16:11 KJV

There is nothing that rejuvenates the parched, delicate spirits of children faster than when a lighthearted spirit pervades the home and laughter fills its halls.

MARCH 11

PROPER RESPECT

He must ... see that his children obey him with proper respect.
1 Timothy 3:4 NIV

When a parent refuses to accept his child's defiant challenge, something changes in their relationship. The youngster begins to look at his mother and father with disrespect; they are unworthy of his allegiance.

MARCH 12

LOVING ONE ANOTHER

Don't criticize and speak evil about each other, dear brothers. If you do, you will be fighting against God's law of loving one another.
James 4:11 TLB

Is your child learning not to gossip and criticize others?

MARCH 13

LOVE AND PROTECTION

He shielded him and cared for him; he guarded him as the apple of his eye, like an eagle that stirs up its nest and hovers over its young, that spreads its wings to catch them and carries them on its pinions.
Deuteronomy 32:10-11 NIV

Parents should be deeply involved in the lives of their young children, providing love and protection and authority. But when those children reach their late teens and early twenties, the cage door must be opened to the world outside.

MARCH 14

CONSISTENT FOUNDATION

But thanks be to God that, though you used to be slaves to sin, you wholeheartedly obeyed the form of teaching to which you were entrusted.
Romans 6:17 NIV

From Genesis to Revelation, there is consistent foundation on which to build an effective philosophy of parent-child relationships.

MARCH 15

ACCOUNTABLE BEFORE GOD

[Jesus] said to them, "Let the little children come to me, and do not hinder them ..." And he took the children in his arms, put his hands on them and blessed them.
Mark 10:14, 16 NIV

Parents are accountable before God to meet their responsibilities to their children, and he is vitally concerned about their welfare.

MARCH 16

TURN TO JESUS

*I am depending on you,
O Lord my God.*
Psalm 7:1 TLB

Does your child see you turn to Jesus for help when you are frightened, anxious, or disturbed?

MARCH 17

WISDOM WILL BE GIVEN YOU

If you want better insight and discernment ... wisdom will be given you.
Proverbs 2:3-5 TLB

You are not to blame for the temperament with which your child was born. He may be a naturally difficult kid to handle, and your task is to rise to the challenge.

MARCH 18

HIS MIGHTY POWER

Glory be to God, who by his mighty power at work within us is able to do far more than we would ever dare to ask or even dream of.
Ephesians 3:20 TLB

God has charged men with the responsibility for providing leadership in their homes and families: in the form of loving authority, financial management, spiritual training, and in the marital relationship.

MARCH 19

WELL-DESERVED PRAISE

Whatever is true, whatever is noble, whatever is right, whatever is pure, whatever is lovely, whatever is admirable – if anything is excellent or praiseworthy – think about such things.
Philippians 4:8 NIV

Parents should always watch for opportunities to offer genuine, well-deserved praise to their children, while avoiding empty flattery.

MARCH 20

FIND REST

*Find rest, O my soul, in God alone;
my hope comes from him. He alone is
my rock and my salvation; he is my
fortress, I will not be shaken.*
Psalm 62:5 NIV

Slow down, what is your rush, anyway? Don't you know your children will be gone so quickly and you will have nothing but blurred memories of those years when they needed you? Once those children are here, they had better fit into our schedule somewhere.

MARCH 21

LET THEM STRUGGLE

For we do not have a high priest who is unable to sympathize with our weaknesses, but we have one who has been tempted in every way, just as we are – yet was without sin.
Hebrews 4:15 NIV

Life inevitably brings pain and sorrow to little people, and we hurt when they hurt. We want to rise like a mighty shield to protect them from life's sting. Yet there are times when we must let them struggle. Children can't grow without taking risks.

MARCH 22

NO PLACE

Quarreling, harsh words, and dislike of others should have no place in your lives.
Ephesians 4:31 TLB

Most emotional disorders (excepting organic illness) can be traced to destructive relationships with people during the first twenty years of life.

MARCH 23

TEACH YOUR CHILDREN

You must think constantly about these commandments I am giving you today. You must teach them to your children and talk about them when you are at home or out for a walk; at bedtime and the first thing in the morning.
Deuteronomy 6:6-7 TLB

The most vital responsibility in parenting – that of introducing our children to Jesus Christ and getting them safely through this dangerous and turbulent world – should be the ultimate goal for every believing parent.

MARCH 24

LEARNING TO CONTROL

For God is at work within you, helping you want to obey him, and then helping you do what he wants.
Philippians 2:13 TLB

Is your child learning to control his impulses?

MARCH 25

DELIBERATE CONTROLS

A life of doing right is the wisest life there is.
Proverbs 4:11 TLB

Sexual contact between a boy and girl is a progressive thing beginning when the relationship is new. They can resist this drift toward intimacy by placing deliberate controls on the physical aspect of their relationship, right from the first date.

MARCH 26

FORGIVE

Bear with each other and forgive whatever grievances you may have against one another. Forgive as the Lord forgave you.
Colossians 3:13 NIV

I am a firm believer in the judicious use of grace (and humour) in parent-child relationships.

MARCH 27

THE CHRISTIAN FAMILY

Anyone who won't care for his own relatives when they need help, especially those living in his own family, has no right to say he is a Christian.
1 Timothy 5:8 TLB

Is your child learning the meaning of the Christian family and the faithfulness to it which God intends?

MARCH 28

ARGUMENTS PRODUCE QUARRELS

Don't have anything to do with foolish and stupid arguments, because you know they produce quarrels. And the Lord's servant must not quarrel.
2 Timothy 2:23-24 NIV

Don't argue with your teen. Don't subject him to perpetual threats and finger-wagging accusations and insulting indictments. And most important, don't nag him endlessly.

MARCH 29

WITHOUT COMPARING

Each one should test his own actions. Then he can take pride in himself, without comparing himself to somebody else.
Galatians 6:4 NIV

Be especially aware of the game called "comparison." It is a killer! I'm convinced that most parents indulge regularly in this practice of comparing their kids with everyone else's.

MARCH 30

ACCEPT YOUR LOT

To enjoy your work and to accept your lot in life – that is indeed a gift from God. The person who does that will not need to look back with sorrow on his past, for God gives him joy.
Ecclesiastes 5:19-20 TLB

To find a satisfactory life's work, answer six questions: (1) What do I like to do? (2) What do I have an opportunity to do? (3) What do I have an ability to do? (4) What can I earn a living doing? (5) What will bring respect from society? (6) What does God want me to do?

MARCH 31

ROD OF CORRECTION

The rod of correction imparts wisdom ... Discipline your son, and he will give you peace; he will bring delight to your soul.
Proverbs 29:15, 17 NIV

Establish boundaries in advance. Tell the child before he breaks the rule just what it is. Make sure he knows what you expect, and why. Punishment is to be reserved for that moment of conflict when the child dares you to defend your right to lead. It should come in response to outright disobedience.

APRIL

APRIL 1

UNDERSTANDING JESUS' DEATH

But God commendeth his love toward us, in that, while we were yet sinners, Christ dies for us.
Romans 5:8 KJV

Without an understanding of the justice of our Creator and of our obligations to serve him – and of his promise to punish wickedness – Jesus' death on the cross is of no consequence. He died to provide a remedy for the curse of sin! Unless one understands the curse, the disease, then there is no need for a cure.

APRIL 2

THERE IS FREEDOM

Now the Lord is the Spirit and where the Spirit of the Lord is, there is freedom.
2 Corinthians 3:17 NIV

Guilt can interfere with a healthy parent-child relationship. It can take the joy out of parenthood, turning the entire responsibility into a painful chore.

APRIL 3

YOUR CONTROLLED RESPONSE

He was brought as a lamb to the slaughter; and as a sheep before her shearers is dumb, so he stood silent before the ones condemning him.
Isaiah 53:7 TLB

Your controlled and loving response to a vicious assault can instantly reveal the Christian values by which you live.

APRIL 4

REAL LOVE IS UNSELFISH

Many waters cannot quench the flame of love, neither can the floods drown it. If a man tried to buy it with everything he owned, he couldn't do it.
Song of Solomon 8:7 TLB

Real love is an expression of the deepest appreciation for another human being; it is an intense awareness of his or her needs and longings – past, present, and future. It is unselfish and giving and caring.

APRIL 5

RETURNED TO THE SHEPHERD

For you were like sheep going astray, but now you have returned to the Shepherd and Overseer of your souls.
1 Peter 2:25 NIV

After punishment, your child will probably want to be loved and reassured. By all means, open your arms and let him come! Hold him close and tell him of your love. Rock him gently and let him know, again, why he was punished and how he can avoid the trouble next time.

APRIL 6

BEHAVIOR AND CONSEQUENCES

"I am he who searches hearts and minds, and I will repay each of you according to your deeds."
Revelation 2:23 NIV

The overall objective during preadolescence is teaching the child that actions have inevitable consequences. One of the most serious casualties in a permissive society is the failure to connect those two factors: behavior and consequences.

APRIL 7

NEGATIVE EMOTIONS

Lord, let your constant love surround us, for our hopes are in you alone.
Psalm 33:22 TLB

If we are to be defeated during life's spiritual pilgrimage, it is likely that negative emotions will play a dominant role in that discouragement. Satan is devastatingly effective in using guilt, rejection, fear, grief, embarrassment, depression, loneliness and misunderstanding.

APRIL 8

LOVING FORGIVENESS

Be ye kind one to another, tenderhearted, forgiving one another, even as God for Christ's sake hath forgiven you.
Ephesians 4:32 KJV

There is always room for more loving forgiveness within our homes.

APRIL 9

LIVE IN COMPLETE HARMONY

May God who gives patience, steadiness, and encouragement help you to live in complete harmony with each other – each with the attitude of Christ toward the other.
Romans 15:5 TLB

All misunderstanding in marriage results from "differing assumptions."

APRIL 10

LOVING FIRMNESS

He who spares the rod hates his son, but he who loves him is careful to discipline him.
Proverbs 13:24 NIV

Corporal punishment is reserved specifically for moments of willful, deliberate, on-purpose defiance by a child who is old enough to understand what he is doing. These challenges to authority should be met with loving firmness.

APRIL 11

ACCEPT INSTRUCTION

Listen to advice and accept instruction, and in the end you will be wise.
Proverbs 19:20 NIV

Grandparents probably should not punish their grandchildren unless the parents have given them permission to do so.

APRIL 12

TO KEEP IN CHECK

We all stumble in many ways. If anyone is never at fault in what he says, he is a perfect man, able to keep his whole body in check.
James 3:2 NIV

If there is one lesson parents need to learn most urgently, it is to guard what they say in the presence of their children.

APRIL 13

A SPIRIT OF SELF-DISCIPLINE

For God did not give us a spirit of timidity, but a spirit of power, of love and of self-discipline.
2 Timothy 1:7 NIV

We adults remember all too clearly the fears and jeers and tears that represented our own tumultuous youth. Perhaps that is why parents begin to quake and tremble when their children approach the adolescent years.

APRIL 14

MEANING IN LIFE

Choose life; that you and your children might live!
Deuteronomy 30:19 TLB

The only true source of meaning in life is found in love for God and his son Jesus Christ, and love for all mankind, beginning with our own families.

APRIL 15

FORMED IN HIS OWN IMAGE

So God created man in his own image, in the image of God he created him; male and female he created them.
Genesis 1:27 NIV

How foolish for us to doubt our value when the Creator formed us in his own image!

APRIL 16

FORGIVE AND FORGET

"If you forgive anyone his sins, they are forgiven; if you do not forgive them, they are not forgiven."
John 20:23 NIV

Is your child learning to forgive and forget?

APRIL 17

LOVE AND DISCIPLINE

Know then in your heart that as a man disciplines his son, so the LORD your God disciplines you.
Deuteronomy 8:5 NIV

The formula of love and discipline has been tested and validated over many centuries of time, and it will work for you.

APRIL 18

A HARVEST OF RIGHTEOUSNESS AND PEACE

No discipline seems pleasant at the time, but painful. Later on, however, it produces a harvest of righteousness and peace for those who have been trained by it.
Hebrews 12:11 NIV

A boy or girl who knows love abounds at home will not resent well-deserved punishment. One who is unloved or ignored will hate any form of discipline!

APRIL 19

BENEVOLENT AUTHORITY

Let us please God by serving him with thankful hearts.
Hebrews 12:28 TLB

Is your child learning that there are many forms of benevolent authority outside himself to which he must submit?

APRIL 20

TO DO YOUR WILL

Teach me to do your will, for you are my God; may your good Spirit lead me on level ground.
Psalm 143:10 NIV

If you permit your youngster's will to remain unbridled, the result is often extreme self-will, which makes him useless to himself, others, or even to God.

APRIL 21

TELL GOD YOUR NEEDS

Don't worry about anything; instead, pray about everything; tell God your needs, and don't forget to thank him for his answers. If you do this, you will experience God's peace, which is far more wonderful than the human mind can understand.
Philippians 4:6-7 TLB

I will make mistakes as a parent. My children will occasionally fall victim to those imperfections. But I cannot abandon my responsibilities to provide leadership simply because I lack infinite wisdom and insight.

APRIL 22

LOVING AUTHORITY

An elder must be blameless, the husband of but one wife, a man whose children believe and are not open to the charge of being wild and disobedient.
Titus 1:6 NIV

Proper authority can be defined as loving leadership. Without decision-makers and others who agree to follow, there is inevitable chaos and confusion and disorder in human relationships. Loving authority is absolutely necessary for the healthy functioning of a family.

APRIL 23

ETERNAL VALUES

The fruit of the righteous is a tree of life, and he who wins souls is wise.
Proverbs 11:30 NIV

When eternal values come in view, our greatest desire is to please the Lord and influence as many of our loved ones for him as possible. If we fully understood that the eternal souls of our children hung in the balance today – that only by winning them for Christ could we spend eternity together in heaven – would we change the way this day is lived?

APRIL 24

LEAD TO RIGHTEOUSNESS

Those who are wise will shine like the brightness of the heavens, and those who lead many to righteousness, like the stars for ever and ever.
Daniel 12:3 NIV

Some children are more sensitive to spiritual matters than others, and they must be allowed to progress at their own pace. But in no sense should we as their parents be casual or neutral about their training. Their world should sparkle with references to Jesus and to our faith.

APRIL 25

THE LORD IS A STRONG TOWER

The name of the LORD is a strong tower; the righteous run to it and are safe.
Proverbs 18:10 NIV

Children derive security from knowing where the boundaries are and who's available to enforce them.

APRIL 26

MY PLACE OF SAFETY

We live within the shadow of the Almighty, sheltered by the God who is above all gods. This I declare, that he alone is my refuge, my place of safety; he is my God, and I am trusting him. For he rescues you from every trap ...
Psalm 91:1-3 TLB

We have systematically been taught to worship beauty and brains. We all want superchildren who will amaze the world. Often the greatest damage (to self-esteem) is unintentionally inflicted right in the home, which should be the child's sanctuary and fortress.

APRIL 27

EVIDENCE OF YOUR FAITH

What is faith? It is the confident assurance that something we want is going to happen. It is the certainty that what we hope for is waiting for us, even though we cannot see it up ahead. Men of God in days of old were famous for their faith.
Hebrews 11:1-2 TLB

Does your child see evidence of your faith in God as you trust him for daily needs and direction?

APRIL 28

ON YOUR GUARD

So be on your guard.
1 Thessalonians 5:6 TLB

The decline of a marriage is rarely brought about by a blowout; it usually falls victim to a slow leak.

APRIL 29

WISE ADVICE

Ability to give wise advice satisfies like a good meal!
Proverbs 18:30 TLB

Parents of compliant children don't understand their friends with defiant youngsters. They intensify guilt and anxiety by implying, "If you would raise your kids the way I do it, you wouldn't be having those problems." May I emphasize to both groups that the willful child can be difficult to handle even when his parents lead him with great skill and dedication.

APRIL 30

THE BENEFIT YOU REAP

Now that you have been set free from sin and have become slaves to God, the benefit you reap leads to holiness, and the result is eternal life. For the wages of sin is death, but the gift of God is eternal life in Christ Jesus our Lord.
Romans 6:22-23 NIV

Every move we make directly affects our future, and irresponsible behavior eventually produces sorrow and pain.

MAY

MAY 1

OUR TENDENCY

He passed in front of Moses, proclaiming, "The LORD, the LORD, the compassionate and gracious God, slow to anger, abounding in love and faithfulness, maintaining love to thousands, and forgiving wickedness, rebellion and sin."
Exodus 34:6-7 NIV

We are not typically kind and loving and generous and yielded to God. Our tendency is toward selfishness and stubbornness and sin. We are all, in effect, "strong-willed children" as we stand before God.

MAY 2

UNCONDITIONAL LOVE

We love because he first loved us.
1 John 4:19 NIV

Unconditional love will heal a troubled home. It will resolve conflicts between parent and child. It will even help us cope with a tragedy.

MAY 3

I WILL REMEMBER

I will remember the deeds of the LORD; yes, I will remember your miracles of long ago. I will meditate on all your works and consider all your mighty deeds.
Psalm 77:11-12 NIV

If we are to understand our children – their feelings and behavior – then we must sharpen our memories of our own childhood.

MAY 4

THE BALANCE

Don't be angry when the Lord punishes you. Don't be discouraged when he has to show you where you are wrong. For when he punishes you, it proves that he loves you.
Hebrews 12:5-6 TLB

The foundational understanding on which the entire parent-child relationship rests is found in a careful balance between love and discipline. The interaction of those two variables is critical and is as close as we can get to a formula for successful parenting.

MAY 5

THE POWER OF PRAYER

This is the confidence we have in approaching God: that if we ask anything according to his will, he hears us.
1 John 5:14 NIV

The solutions to the problems of modern parenthood can be found through the power of prayer and personal appeal to the Creator.

MAY 6

THE MEANING OF FAITH AND TRUST

*Those who trust in the Lord
are steady as Mount Zion,
unmoved by any circumstance.*
Psalm 125:1 TLB

Is your child learning the meaning of faith and trust?

MAY 7

SET THEM AN EXAMPLE

In everything set them an example by doing what is good.
Titus 2:7 NIV

Children miss nothing in sizing up their parents. If you are only half convinced of your beliefs, they will quickly discern that fact. Any ethical weak spot — any indecision on your part — will be incorporated and then magnified in your sons and daughters. Their faith or faithlessness will be a reflection of our own.

MAY 8

A GOOD MOTHER

Her children stand and bless her; so does her husband. He praises her with these words: "There are many fine women in the world, but you are the best of them all!"
Proverbs 31:28-29 TLB

Being a good mother is one of the most complex skills in life. What activity could be more important than shaping human lives during their impressionable and plastic years?

MAY 9

THY WORD

*Thy word is a lamp unto my feet,
and a light unto my path.*
Psalm 119:105 KJV

I'm convinced that self-esteem has more frequently been assassinated over reading problems than any other aspect of school life. And it is all so unnecessary! Every child, with very few exceptions, can learn to read if taught properly.

MAY 10

YOUR WORDS

Nothing is perfect except your words.
Psalm 119:96 TLB

Does your child see and hear you using Scripture in daily life – applying it, quoting it, emphasizing its significance and meaning?

MAY 11

HUMAN WORTH

God ... has blessed us in the heavenly realms with every spiritual blessing in Christ.
Ephesians 1:3 NIV

Human worth does not depend on beauty or intelligence or accomplishments. We are all more valuable than the possessions of the entire world, simply because God gave us that value. This fact remains true, even if every other person on earth treats us like losers.

MAY 12

A SOLID SPIRITUAL FOUNDATION

You are no longer foreigners and aliens, but fellow citizens with God's people and members of God's household, built on the foundation of the apostles and prophets, with Christ Jesus himself as the chief cornerstone.
Ephesians 2:19-20 NIV

Parents who recognize the inevitable war between good and evil will do their best to influence the child's choices – to shape his will and provide a solid spiritual foundation.

MAY 13

QUESTIONS ABOUT GOD

The Lord who gives us sunlight in the daytime and the moon and stars to light the night ... stirs the sea to make the roaring waves – his name is Lord Almighty.
Jeremiah 31:35 TLB

Children need adults who can go for casual walks and talk about fishing, to look at pretty leaves and caterpillars ... and answer questions about God and the nature of the world as it is.

MAY 14

I ACKNOWLEDGED MY SIN

Day and night your hand was heavy upon me; my strength was sapped as in the heat of summer. Then I acknowledged my sin to you and did not cover up my iniquity.
Psalm 32:4-5 NIV

Be willing to let your child experience a reasonable amount of pain or inconvenience when he behaves irresponsibly.

MAY 15

FROM INFANCY YOU HAVE KNOWN

But as for you, continue in what you have learned and have become convinced of, because you know those from whom you learned it, and how from infancy you have known the holy Scriptures, which are able to make you wise for salvation ...
2 Timothy 3:14-15 NIV

Human mental awakening is thrilling. Every day, something new is learned. This normal process is exciting, especially for those who are watching for the first time.

MAY 16

THE DILIGENT PROSPER

Lazy people want much but get little, while the diligent are prospering.
Proverbs 13:4 TLB

Is your child learning to work and carry responsibility?

MAY 17

GOOD GIFTS

If you, then, though you are evil, know how to give good gifts to your children, how much more will your Father in heaven give good gifts to those who ask him!
Matthew 7:11 NIV

We parents, in our great love for our children, can do irreparable harm by yielding to their pleas for more and more things. There are times when the very best reply we can offer is ... no.

MAY 18

ADOLESCENT SENSES

How can a young man keep his way pure? By living according to your word.
Psalm 119:9 NIV

Most students will go through an academic valley sometime between the sixth and ninth grades in school. The reason is the massive assault made on adolescent senses by the growing-up process. Selfconfidence is shaken to the foundation. Happy hormones crank into action. Who can think about school with all that going on?

MAY 19

DIGNITY AND WORTH

For you created my inmost being; you knit me together in my mother's womb. I praise you because I am fearfully and wonderfully made; your works are wonderful, I know that full well.
Psalm 139:13-14 NIV

We all have human worth, yet so many young people conclude that they're somehow different — that they're truly inferior — that they lack the necessary ingredients for dignity and worth.

MAY 20

HONESTY

The Lord hates cheating and delights in honesty.
Proverbs 11:1 TLB

Is your child learning to be truthful and honest?

MAY 21

LOVE AND DIGNITY

But the fruit of the Spirit is love, joy, peace, patience, kindness, goodness, faithfulness, gentleness and self-control.
Galations 5:22-23 NIV

Adults should devote their creative energies to the teaching of love and dignity. And if necessary, we should insist that children approach each other with kindness.

MAY 22

PERSONAL WORTH

Be strong and very courageous. Be careful to obey all the law my servant Moses gave you; do not turn from it to the right or to the left, that you may be successful wherever you go.
Joshua 1:7 NIV

The slow learner needs parental help in finding his compensating skills, coupled with the assurance that his personal worth does not depend on success in academia.

MAY 23

I WILL SUSTAIN YOU

Even to your old age and gray hairs I am he, I am he who will sustain you. I have made you and I will carry you; I will sustain you and I will rescue you.
Isaiah 46:4 NIV

You can make it through the most difficult of experiences, and even though it feels like God is unconcerned, he really does care!

MAY 24

THE WAGES OF SIN

LORD, I have heard of your fame; I stand in awe of your deeds, O LORD. Renew them in our day, in our time make them known; in wrath remember mercy.
Habakkuk 3:2 NIV

The universe is ordered by a supreme Lord who requires obedience from his children and has warned them that the "wages of sin is death." To show our little ones love without authority is as serious a distortion of God's nature as to reveal an ironfisted authority without love.

MAY 25

KEEP THE SABBATH DAY HOLY

*Remember the Sabbath
day by keeping it holy.*
Exodus 20:8 NIV

Is your child learning to keep the Sabbath day holy?

MAY 26

WILLING TO SHARE

Command them to do good, to be rich in good deeds, and to be generous and willing to share. In this way they will lay up treasure for themselves.
1 Timothy 6:18-19 NIV

Don't saturate your child with materialism. There are few conditions that inhibit a sense of appreciation more than for a child to feel he is entitled to whatever he wants, whenever he wants it.

MAY 27

BY MY SPIRIT

"Not by might nor by power, but by my Spirit," says the LORD Almighty.
Zechariah 4:6 NIV

I am not critical of the motives behind what might be called "super-parenting." Children are worth our very best efforts to raise them properly. Nevertheless, even a noble and necessary task can be taken to such extremes that it becomes harmful to both the giver and the receiver.

MAY 28

SELF-ESTEEM

We will tell the next generation the praiseworthy deeds of the LORD, his power, and the wonders he has done.
Psalm 78:4 NIV

A popular theme in recent literature has been, "How to be a good parent in your spare time," appealing to this notion that effective childrearing is duck soup for the parent who organizes and delegates properly. But the building of self-esteem in your child is one responsibility that cannot be delegated to others.

MAY 29

TRIALS TO TEST YOUR FAITH

These trials are only to test your faith, to see whether or not it is strong and pure.
1 Peter 1:7 TLB

Sincere, dedicated believers go through tunnels and storms, too. We inflict a tremendous disservice on young Christians by making them think only sinners experience confusion and depressing times in their lives.

MAY 30

RESPECT OTHER PEOPLE

Live as servants of God. Show proper respect to everyone: Love the brotherhood of believers.
1 Peter 2:16-17 NIV

Loving discipline encourages a child to respect other people and live as a responsible, constructive citizen.

MAY 31

WITHIN THE BOUNDARIES

Stay always within the boundaries where God's love can reach and bless you.
Jude 1:21 TLB

Strong desire is like a river. As long as it flows within the banks of God's will – be the current strong or weak – all is well. But when it floods over those boundaries and seeks its own channels, then disaster lurks in the rampage below.

JUNE

JUNE 1

AT A PRICE

You are not your own; you were bought at a price.
1 Corinthians 6:20 NIV

Everything worth having comes with a price. If improvement is to be made in the development of mental skills and knowledge, it will be accomplished through blood, sweat, and a few tears.

JUNE 2

IMITATORS OF GOD

Be imitators of God, therefore, as dearly loved children and live a life of love, just as Christ loved us and gave himself up for us as a fragrant offering and sacrifice to God.
Ephesians 5:1-2 NIV

The Creator has given to us parents the awesome responsibility of representing him to our children. Our heavenly Father is a God of unlimited love, and our children must become acquainted with his mercy and tenderness through our own love toward them.

JUNE 3

PRESERVE SOUND JUDGMENT

My son, preserve sound judgment and discernment, do not let them out of your sight ... Then you will go on your way in safety, and your foot will not stumble.
Proverbs 3:21, 23 NIV

Certain risks must be tolerated if a child is to learn and progress; he will never learn to walk if he is not allowed to fall down in the process.

JUNE 4

THE GOOD OF OTHERS

Nobody should seek his own good, but the good of others.
1 Corinthians 10:24 NIV

Is your child learning not to be selfish and demanding?

JUNE 5

REJECTED BEHAVIOUR

*I will heal their waywardness and
love them freely, for my anger
has turned away from them.*
Hosea 14:4 NIV

Parental warmth after discipline is essential to demonstrate that it is the behavior – not the child himself – that the parent rejects.

JUNE 6

A MAN'S CONSCIENCE

A man's conscience is the Lord's searchlight exposing his hidden motives.
Proverbs 20:27 TLB

Is your child learning to follow the dictates of his own conscience?

JUNE 7

GOD HEARS YOUR PETITIONS

Ask, and you will be given what you ask for.
Matthew 7:7 TLB

Hold your children before the Lord in fervent prayer throughout their years at home. There is no other source of confidence and wisdom in parenting. The God who made your children will hear your petitions. He has promised to do so.

JUNE 8

CONTENTMENT

I have learned the secret of being content in any and every situation, whether well fed or hungry, whether living in plenty or in want.
Philippians 4:12 NIV

Men and women should recognize that dissatisfaction with life can become nothing more than a bad habit – a costly attitude that can rob them of life's pleasures.

JUNE 9

CAST YOUR ANXIETY ON HIM

*Cast all your anxiety on him
because he cares for you.*
1 Peter 5:7 NIV

Parenthood can sometimes be a very guilt-producing affair. Even when we give it our best effort, we can see our own failures and mistakes reflected in the lives of our children.

JUNE 10

LEARNING TO SHARE

Don't forget to do good and to share what you have.
Hebrews 13:16 TLB

Is your child learning to share?

JUNE 11

CARRY IT ON TO COMPLETION

In all my prayers for all of you, I always pray with joy ... being confident of this, that he who began a good work in you will carry it on to completion until the day of Christ Jesus.
Philippians 1:4, 6 NIV

The objective is to take the raw material with which our babies arrive on this earth and then gradually mold it into mature, responsible, and God-fearing adults.

JUNE 12

EMPATHIZE WITH LITTLE PEOPLE

All of you, live in harmony with one another; be sympathetic, love as brothers, be compassionate and humble.
1 Peter 3:8 NIV

Parents and teachers can contribute greatly to the self-respect of the next generation if they can genuinely empathize with little people – seeing what they see, hearing what they hear, and feeling what they feel.

JUNE 13

LOVING AUTHORITY

If anyone obeys his word, God's love is truly made complete in him. This is how we know we are in him: Whoever claims to live in him must walk as Jesus did.
1 John 2:5-6 NIV

Why is parental authority so vigorously supported throughout the Bible? The leadership of parents plays a significant role in the development of a child. By learning to yield to the loving authority (leadership) of his parents, a child learns to submit to other forms of authority that will confront him later in life.

JUNE 14

CITIZENSHIP IN HEAVEN

But our citizenship is in heaven. And we eagerly await a Savior from there, the Lord Jesus Christ.
Philippians 3:20 NIV

If it is important to produce respectful, responsible young citizens, then we should set out to mold them accordingly.

JUNE 15

FULLY TRAINED

*Everyone who is fully trained
will be like his teacher.*
Luke 6:40 NIV

A child should be exposed to a carefully conceived, systematic program of religious training. Yet we are much too haphazard about this matter. Perhaps we would hit the mark more often if we more clearly recognize the precise target.

JUNE 16

SLEEP IN PEACE

I will lie down and sleep in peace, for you alone, O LORD, make me dwell in safety.
Psalm 4:8 NIV

Don't deal with big problems late at night. A good night's sleep and a rich cup of coffee can go a long way toward defusing the problem.

JUNE 17

UNDERSTAND AND EMPATHIZE

Kneeling beside him the Samaritan soothed his wounds with medicine and bandaged them. Then he put the man on his donkey and walked along beside him till they came to an inn, where he nursed him through the night.
Luke 10:34 TLB

Is your child learning to understand and empathize with the feelings of others?

JUNE 18

GOOD JUDGMENT

Those who hope in the LORD will renew their strength. They will soar on wings like eagles; they will run and not grow weary, they will walk and not be faint.
Isaiah 40:31 NIV

Burnout is an occupational hazard for Christian parents. Superparenting is a natural trap for them. The family ranks near the top of our value system, and our way of life focuses on self-sacrifice and commitment to others. It can be a trap when applied without good judgment at home.

JUNE 19

A REWARD FROM HIM

Sons are a heritage from the LORD, children a reward from him. Like arrows in the hands of a warrior are sons born in one's youth. Blessed is the man whose quiver is full of them.
Psalm 127:3-5 NIV

The goal of proper child rearing is not to produce perfect kids. Even if you implement a flawless system of discipline at home, which no one in history has done, your children will be children.

JUNE 20

THE VITAL TASK

*Perseverance must finish its
work so that you may be
mature, not lacking anything.*
James 1:4 NIV

The vital task of turning a child loose is important all the way through his march toward young adulthood. Each year he should make more of his own decisions than in the prior twelve months; the routine responsibilities of living should fall to his shoulders as he is able to handle them.

JUNE 21

SELF-DISCIPLINE AND CONTROL

For the grace of God that brings salvation has appeared to all men. It teaches us to say "No" to ungodliness and worldly passions, and to live self-controlled, upright and godly lives in this present age.
Titus 2:11-12 NIV

One of the purposes of education is to prepare the young for later life. It takes a good measure of self-discipline and control to cope with the demands of modern living.

JUNE 22

DO NOT GROW WEARY

Let us fix our eyes on Jesus, the author and perfecter of our faith, who for the joy set before him endured the cross, scorning its shame, and sat down at the right hand of the throne of God. Consider him who endured such opposition from sinful men, so that you will not grow weary and lose heart.
Hebrews 12:2-3

We live in a very hectic period of history, where fatigue and time pressure are our worst enemies.

JUNE 23

PEACE OF MIND

Who of you by worrying can add a single hour to his life?
Matthew 6:27 NIV

Life has enough crises in it without magnifying our troubles during good times, yet peace of mind is often surrendered for such insignificant causes.

JUNE 24

TRAINING IN RESPONSIBILITY

Fathers, do not exasperate your children; instead, bring them up in the training and instruction of the Lord.
Ephesians 6:4 NIV

The best preparation for responsible adulthood is derived from proper training in responsibility during childhood. The child can be encouraged to progress on an orderly timetable of events, carrying the level of responsibility that is appropriate for his age.

JUNE 25

THE INTERPRETATION OF MEANING

Know thou the God of thy father, and serve him with a perfect heart and with a willing mind: for the Lord searcheth all hearts, and understandeth all the imaginations of the thoughts.
1 Chronicles 28:9 KJV

The most effective parents are those who can get behind the eyes of their child, seeing what he sees, thinking what he thinks, feeling what he feels. The art of good parenthood revolves around the interpretation of meaning behind behaviour.

JUNE 26

LIVE HAPPILY WITH THE WOMAN YOU LOVE

Live happily with the woman you love through the fleeting days of life, for the wife God gives you is your best reward down here for all your earthly toil.
Ecclesiastes 9:9 TLB

Many (if not most) marriages suffer from a failure to recognize a universal characteristic of human nature. We value that which we are fortunate to get; we discredit that with which we are stuck!

JUNE 27

MAKE MUSIC TO THE LORD

Speak to one another with psalms, hymns and spiritual songs. Sing and make music in your heart to the Lord, always giving thanks to God.
Ephesians 5:19-20 NIV

Stay involved as a family in a church that meets your needs and preaches the Word. We are designed to love God and to love one another. To be deprived of either function can be devastating.

JUNE 28

ACCEPT THE INEVITABLE

*In repentance and rest is
your salvation, in quietness
and trust is your strength.*
Isaiah 30:15 NIV

Don't struggle with things you can't change. The first principle of mental health is to learn to accept the inevitable. To do otherwise is to run with the brakes on.

JUNE 29

FIGHT FOR WHAT YOU BELIEVE

Obey the government, for God is the one who has put it there. There is no government anywhere that God has not placed in power.
Romans 13:1 TLB

A save the family project: Join your political party's local precinct committee in order to fight for what you believe.

JUNE 30

HIS DIVINE POWER

His divine power has given us everything we need for life and godliness through our knowledge of him who called us by his own glory and goodness.
2 Peter 1:3 NIV

It is obvious that the Creator of the universe is best able to tell us how to raise children, and he has done just that through his Holy Word.

JULY

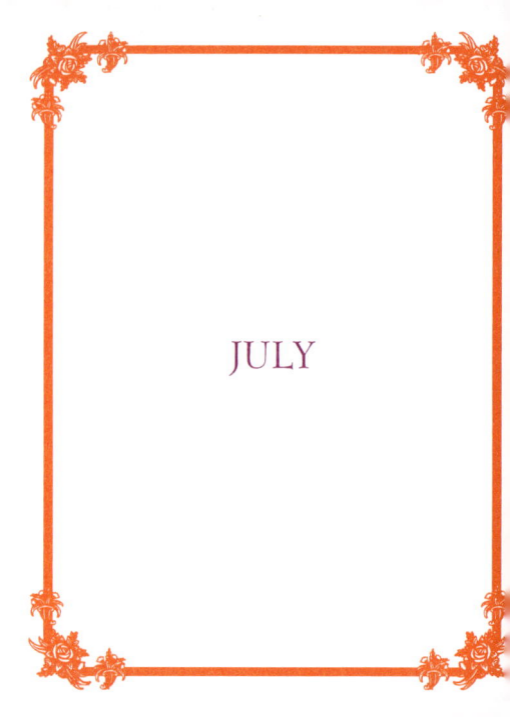

JULY 1

BECAUSE YOU ARE YOUNG

Don't let anyone look down on you because you are young, but set an example for the believers.
1 Timothy 4:12 NIV

Adolescence is not a physical term. It does not mean "the time of life when a child matures sexually." That is the definition of "puberty." Adolescence is a cultural term, meaning the age between childhood and adulthood when an individual neither has the privileges of childhood nor the freedom of adulthood.

JULY 2

DEMAND FOR ENERGY

We pray ... that you may live a life worthy of the Lord and may please him in every way: bearing fruit in every good work, growing in the knowledge of God, being strengthened ... so that you may have great endurance and patience.
Colossians 1:10-11 NIV

The society in which we live places heavy demands on us. Something has to give. When the demand for energy exceeds the supply, burnout is inevitable. And children are almost always the losers in the competition for that limited resource.

JULY 3

A TIME FOR EVERYTHING

There is a time for everything ... a time to be silent and a time to speak.
Ecclesiastes 3:1, 7 NIV

There may be a time and place for strong feelings to be expressed and there will be occasions for quiet tolerance.

JULY 4

GRANTING INDEPENDENCE

I have been crucified with Christ and I no longer live, but Christ lives in me. The life I live in the body, I live by faith in the Son of God, who loved me and gave himself for me.
Galatians 2:20 NIV

Begin releasing your children during the preschool years, granting independence that is consistent with their age and maturity. Each year, more responsibility and freedom (they are companions) are given to the child.

JULY 5

SELF-ESTEEM

Do not let any unwholesome talk come out of your mouths, but only what is helpful for building others up according to their needs, that it may benefit those who listen.
Ephesians 4:29 NIV

Self-esteem is the most fragile attribute in human nature. It can be damaged by very minor incidents, and its reconstruction is often difficult to engineer.

JULY 6

BOW IN REVERENCE

His joy is in those who reverence him, those who expect him to be loving and kind.
Psalm 147:11 TLB

Is your child learning to bow in reverence before the God of the universe?

JULY 7

A GOOD SELF-CONCEPT

Oh, how delightful you are; how pleasant.
Song of Solomon 7:6 TLB

Love from her husband is linked to self-esteem in a wife. It is her lifeblood. For a husband, however, romantic experiences with his wife are warm, enjoyable, and memorable – but not necessary to a good self-concept. This is an important distinction between the sexes.

JULY 8

BE STILL

Be still, and know that I am God.
Psalm 46:10 NIV

Creativity can flourish only when there's enough order in the classroom to allow for concentrated thought. Chaos and creativity don't mix.

JULY 9

ACKNOWLEDGE INNER THOUGHTS

All my longings lie open before you, O Lord; my sighing is not hidden from you.
Psalm 38:9 NIV

Most discouraged young people will not admit how they feel because it hurts to acknowledge these inner thoughts.

JULY 10

THE STABILITY OF HOME AND FAMILY

I will not forget you! See, I have engraved you on the palms of my hands; your walls are ever before me.
Isaiah 49:15-16 NIV

I cannot overemphasize the importance of parental support and love during the formative years of life. A child's sense of security and well-being is primarily rooted in the stability of his home and family.

JULY 11

TIME TOGETHER

He who finds a wife finds what is good and receives favor from the Lord.
Proverbs 18:22 NIV

A husband and wife should have a date every week or two, leaving the children at home and forgetting the day's problems for an evening.

JULY 12

CELEBRATE YOUR UNIQUENESS

Remember that in God's plan men and women need each other.
1 Corinthians 11:11 TLB

Males and females are different. God authored those differences and we should appreciate them. It is our uniqueness that gives freshness and vitality to a relationship. Celebrate your uniqueness and learn to compromise whenever male and female individuality collide.

JULY 13

IN NO WAY BE ASHAMED

I eagerly expect and hope that I will in no way be ashamed, but will have sufficient courage so that now as always Christ will be exalted in my body, whether by life or by death.
Philippians 1:20 NIV

Every pre-teenager should be informed of the rapid changes that are about to occur within his body. The doubts and fears are endless, yet they could be avoided by healthy, confident parental instruction.

JULY 14

TREAT WITH DIGNITY

In humility consider others better than yourselves. Each of you should look not only to your own interests, but also to the interests of others.
Philippians 2:3-4 NIV

Parents cannot require their children to treat them with dignity if they will not do the same in return. They should be gentle with their child's ego, never belittling or embarrassing him or her in front of friends.

JULY 15

PRIDE ENDS IN A FALL

Pride ends in a fall, while humility brings honor.
Proverbs 29:23 TLB

Is your child already learning the vast difference between self-worth and egotistical pride?

JULY 16

PERSEVERE

Blessed is the man who perseveres under trial, because when he has stood the test, he will receive the crown of life that God has promised to those who love him.
James 1:12 NIV

I offer this advice to parents of teenagers: "Get 'em through it." Normality will return eventually if you don't turn the boat over. That may not sound like such a stunning idea, but I believe it has merit for most families – especially those with one or more tough-minded kids.

JULY 17

THE COURAGE TO SEEK THE BEST

We know and rely on the love God has for us. God is love. Whoever lives in love lives in God, and God in him. In this way, love is made complete among us so that we will have confidence on the day of judgement, because in this world we are like him.
1 John 4:16-17 NIV

Our youngsters need not hide in shame; we can give them the courage to seek the best from their world.

JULY 18

TEMPLE FOR GOD

We who believe are carefully joined together with Christ as parts of a beautiful, constantly growing temple for God.
Ephesians 2:21 TLB

Is your child learning to behave properly in church – God's house?

JULY 19

A COMMITMENT OF THE WILL

But as for me and my household, we will serve the Lord.
Joshua 24:15 NIV

Love is more than a feeling – it also involves a commitment of the will. You need an iron-fisted determination to make your marriage succeed, which will act like the engine of a train. It will keep you moving down the right track. On the other hand, the feeling of love is like a caboose, being pulled by the powerful engine at the other end.

JULY 20

A TIME TO EVERY PURPOSE

To every thing there is a season, and a time to every purpose under the heaven ... A time to weep, and a time to laugh; a time to mourn, and a time to dance.
Ecclesiastes 3:1, 4 KJV

Give your child an exposure to responsibility and work, but preserve time for play and fun.

JULY 21

"YES" IN CHRIST

For no matter how many promises God has made, they are "Yes" in Christ.
2 Corinthians 1:20 NIV

While every child needs to be acquainted with denial of some of his more extravagant wishes, there is also a need for parents to consider each request on its own merit. There are so many necessary "no's" in life that we should say "yes" whenever we can.

JULY 22

LET THE MORNING BRING ME WORD

Let the morning bring me word of your unfailing love, for I have put my trust in you. Show me the way I should go, for to you I lift up my soul.
Psalm 143:8 NIV

Make no important, life-shaping decisions quickly or impulsively, and when in doubt, stall for time.

JULY 23

APPROPRIATE PUNISHMENT

Blessed is the man whom God corrects; so do not despise the discipline of the Almighty.
Job 5:17 NIV

Disciplinary action is not an assault on parental love; it is a function of it. Appropriate punishment is not something parents do *to* a beloved child; it is something done *for* him or her.

JULY 24

AN INTERESTING CONSEQUENCE

The character of even a child can be known by the way he acts – whether what he does is pure and right.
Proverbs 20:11 TLB

Statistical records indicate that our children are growing taller today than in the past, probably resulting from better nutrition, medicine, exercise, rest, and recreation. And this additional stature has produced an interesting consequence: sexual maturity is ocurring at younger and younger ages.

JULY 25

DO NOT GIVE UP

Let us not become weary in doing good, for at the proper time we will reap a harvest if we do not give up.
Galatians 6:9 NIV

An adolescent turns the house upside down – literally and figuratively. Not only is the typical rebellion of those years an extremely stressful experience, but the chauffeuring, supervising, cooking and cleaning required to support an adolescent can be exhausting.

JULY 26

OUR LORD WILL GUIDE OUR STEPS

I will bless the Lord who counsels me; he gives me wisdom in the night. He tells me what to do.
Psalm 16:7 TLB

Like a father leading his trusting child, our Lord will guide our steps and teach us his wisdom.

JULY 27

RESERVE TIME FOR YOURSELF

*My soul finds rest in God alone;
my salvation comes from him.*
Psalm 62:1 NIV

Reserve some time for yourself. It is unhealthy for anyone to work all the time.

JULY 28

PRECEPTS AND VALUES

*This has been my practice:
I obey your precepts.*
Psalm 119:56 NIV

Do you want to help your children reach the maximum potential that lies within them? Then raise them according to the precepts and values given to us in the Scriptures.

JULY 29

TWO CAN ACCOMPLISH MORE

Two can accomplish more than twice as much as one, for the results can be much better. If one falls, the other pulls him up; but if a man falls when he is alone, he's in trouble.
Ecclesiates 4:9-10 TLB

Lasting love and affection often develop between people who have survived a crisis together.

JULY 30

KEEP THE SABBATH HOLY

If you keep the Sabbath holy ... honoring the Lord in what you do, not following your own desires and pleasure nor talking idly – then the Lord will be your delight.
Isaiah 58:13-14 TLB

Does your child see you planning your Sunday activities so that they will honor God?

JULY 31

LOVE IS KIND

Love is patient, love is kind. It does not envy, it does not boast, it is not proud. It is not rude, it is not self-seeking, it is not easily angered, it keeps no record of wrongs.
1 Corinthians 13:4-5 NIV

Love is not grabbing, or selfish or self-centered. Real love is being able to contribute to the happiness of another person without expecting to get anything in return.

AUGUST

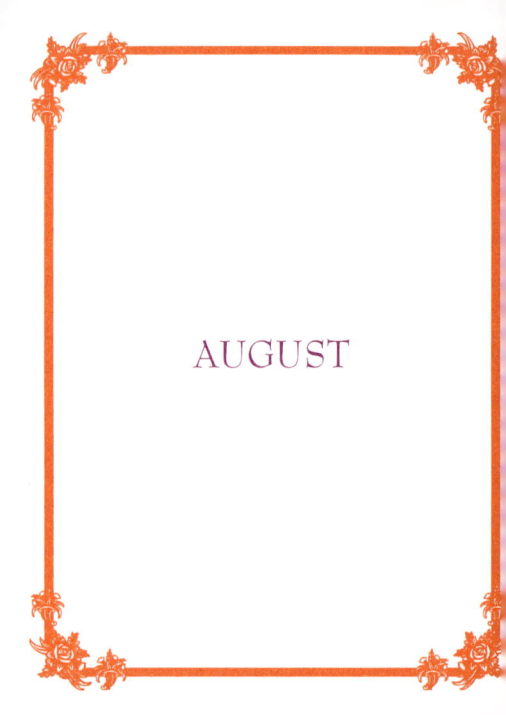

AUGUST 1

CHRIST'S AMBASSADORS

We are therefore Christ's ambassadors, as though God were making his appeal through us.
2 Corinthians 5:20 NIV

God has given us the assignment of representing Him during the formative years of parenting. That's why it is so critically important for us to acquaint our children with God's two predominant natures, His justice and his unfathomable love.

AUGUST 2

THE PRINCIPLE OF PARENTING

It is best to listen much, speak little, and not become angry.
James 1:19 TLB

The overriding principle of parenting remains the same: it involves discipline with love, a reasonable introduction to responsibility and self-control, parental leadership with a minimum of anger, respect for the dignity of the child, realistic boundaries that are enforced with confident firmness, and a judicious use of rewards and punishment.

AUGUST 3

YOUR ARE WORTH MORE

Are not two sparrows sold for a penny? Yet not one of them will fall to the ground apart from the will of your Father ... So don't be afraid; you are worth more than many sparrows.
Matthew 10:29, 31 NIV

Once a child begins to think he's stupid, incapable, ignorant, or foolish, the concept is not easily eliminated.

AUGUST 4

LEARNING TO PRAY

This is the prayer he taught them ...
Luke 11:2 TLB

Is your child learning to pray?

AUGUST 5

FREEDOM TO LOVE

You have been given freedom: not freedom to do wrong, but freedom to love and serve each other.
Galatians 5:13 TLB

The quickest way to destroy a romantic love between a husband and wife is for one partner to clamp a steel cage around the other.

AUGUST 6

BUILD EACH OTHER UP

Therefore encourage one another and build each other up.
1 Thessalonians 5:11 NIV

It isn't often a father says something that he considers profound to his teenage son. Opportunities for that kind of communication have to be created. And it's worth working to achieve.

AUGUST 7

BUILDING FRIENDSHIPS

May the God who gives endurance and encouragement give you a spirit of unity among yourselves as you follow Christ Jesus, so that with one heart and mouth you may glorify the God and Father of our Lord Jesus Christ.
Romans 15:5-6 NIV

Many confrontations can be avoided by building friendships with kids and thereby making them want to cooperate at home. It sure beats anger as a motivator!

AUGUST 8

NOT ASHAMED

Do your best to present yourself to God as one approved, a workman who does not need to be ashamed.
2 Timothy 2:15 NIV

I have seen parents get "hurt" because their developing teenager suddenly seemed embarrassed to be with them. They are not really ashamed of their parents; they are embarrassed by the adult-baby role that was more appropriate in prior years. Parents would do well to accept this healthy aspect of growing up without becoming defensive about it.

AUGUST 9

RELATED TO ONE ANOTHER

May God prosper you and your family and multiply everything you own.
1 Samuel 25:6 TLB

The traditional definition of the family? It is a group of individuals who are related to one another by marriage, birth, or adoption – nothing more, nothing less.

AUGUST 10

THE PARENT-CHILD RELATIONSHIP

Train a child in the way he should go, and when he is old he will not turn from it.
Proverbs 22:6 NIV

The parent-child relationship is the first and most important social interaction a youngster will have, and the flaws and knots experienced there can often be seen later in life.

AUGUST 11

THE RIGHT DIRECTION

Respect those who work hard among you ... Hold them in the highest regard in love because of their work.
1 Thessalonians 5:12-13 NIV

The Lord will place key individuals in the paths of our sons and daughters for whom we pray – people of influence who can nudge them in the right direction when they are beyond the reach of our leadership.

AUGUST 12

A SAFE ATMOSPHERE

The fruit of righteousness will be peace; the effect of righteousness will be quietness and confidence forever. My people will live in peaceful dwelling places, in secure homes, in undisturbed places of rest.
Isaiah 32:17-18 NIV

Children love good disciplinarians primarily because they are afraid of each other and want the security of a leader who can provide a safe atmosphere. Anything can happen in the absence of adult leadership.

AUGUST 13

LOVE MUST BE FED

Speaking the truth in love, we will in all things grow up into him who is the Head, that is, Christ. From him the whole body, joined and held together by every supporting ligament, grows and builds itself up in love.
Ephesians 4:15-16 NIV

Love must be supported and fed and protected, just like a little infant who is growing up at home.

AUGUST 14

AT THE CROSSROADS

This is what the LORD says: "Stand at the crossroads and look; ask for the ancient paths, ask where the good way is, and walk in it, and you will find rest for your souls."
Jeremiah 6:16 NIV

God in his love gave Adam and Eve a choice between good and evil and they abused it. Will he now withhold that same freedom from your children? No. Ultimately, they will decide for themselves.

AUGUST 15

ALLOWED BY INDULGENCE

Can the Ethiopian change his skin or the leopard its spots? Neither can you do good who are accustomed to doing evil.
Jeremiah 13:23 NIV

If the strong-willed child is allowed by indulgence to develop "habits" of defiance and disrespect during his early childhood, those characteristics will haunt him for the next twenty years.

AUGUST 16

CONTROLLED BY THE SPIRIT

*The mind controlled by
the Spirit is life and peace.*
Romans 8:6 NIV

Husbands and wives should constantly guard against the scourge of overcommitment. Even worthwhile and enjoyable activities become damaging when they consume the last ounce of energy or the remaining free moments in the day.

AUGUST 17

CORRECT YOUR CHILDREN

Don't fail to correct your children; discipline won't hurt them!
Proverbs 23:13-14 TLB

A spanking is to be reserved for use in response to willful defiance rather than mere childish irresponsibility.

AUGUST 18

SELF-AWARENESS

*Let your eyes look straight ahead,
fix your gaze directly before you.
Make level paths for your feet and
take only ways that are firm.*
Proverbs 4:25-26 NIV

The child with a good sense of identity is acquainted with his own goals, strengths, weaknesses, desires, hopes and dreams. A child who has been given meaningful self-awareness by his parents and teachers knows where he's going. He is a fortunate individual in this day of gray, indistinct self-awareness.

AUGUST 19

THE DESIRE FOR CONTROL

People will love only themselves and their money; they will be proud and boastful, sneering at God, disobedient to their parents, ungrateful to them, and thoroughly bad.
2 Timothy 3:2 TLB

The desire for control appears to have its roots in the early hours after birth. Even mature adults are usually involved in power games with other people. It happens whenever human interests collide, but it is especially prevalent in families.

AUGUST 20

DIVINE FORGIVENESS

If we confess our sins, he is faithful and just to forgive us our sins, and to cleanse us from all unrighteousness.
1 John 1:9 KJV

After a time of conflict it is extremely important to pray with the child, admitting to God that we have all sinned and no one is perfect. Divine forgiveness is a marvelous experience, even for a very young child.

AUGUST 21

KEEP MY COMMANDS

Oh, that their hearts would be inclined to fear me and keep all my commands always, so that it might go well with them and their children forever!
Deuteronomy 5:29 NIV

Your contributions to your children and grandchildren could rank as your greatest accomplishments in life – or your most oppressive failures.

AUGUST 22

SEARCH FOR AREAS OF AGREEMENT

Each one of you also must love his wife as he loves himself, and the wife must respect her husband.
Ephesians 5:33 NIV

Both a good marriage and a bad marriage have moments of struggle, but in a healthy relationship the husband and wife search for answers and areas of agreement because they love each other.

AUGUST 23

NO CONDEMNATION

Therefore, there is now no condemnation for those who are in Christ Jesus.
Romans 8:1 NIV

God takes our parenting tasks seriously and expects us to do likewise. But he does not intend for us to grovel in guilt for circumstances beyond our control!

AUGUST 24

RUN STRAIGHT TO THE GOAL

I run straight to the goal with purpose in every step. I fight to win. I'm not just shadow-boxing or playing around.
1 Corinthians 9:26 TLB

Relay races are won or lost in the transfer of the baton. According to the Christian values that govern my life, my most important reason for living is to get the baton – the gospel of Jesus Christ – safely in the hands of my children.

AUGUST 25

PROPER PERSPECTIVE

Let the wise listen and add to their learning ... The fear of the LORD is the beginning of knowledge.
Proverbs 1:5, 7 NIV

Education is important today, and we want our children to go as far as they can academically. But let's keep our goals in proper perspective. It is possible that the low achiever will outperform the academic superstar in the long run.

AUGUST 26

THIS PERCEPTIVE SKILL

Carry each other's burdens, and in this way you will fulfill the law of Christ.
Galatians 6:2 NIV

It is an awareness of his work that permits a parent to hold the child when he is threatened, or love him when he is lonely, or teach him when he is inquisitive, or discipline him when he knows he is wrong. The success of the entire parent-child relationship depends on this perceptive skill.

AUGUST 27

LOVE NEVER FAILS

Love does not delight in evil but rejoices with the truth. It always protects, always trusts, always hopes, always perseveres. Love never fails.
1 Corinthians 13:6-8 NIV

Genuine love is focused on another human being. It brings a deep desire to make that person happy ... to meet their needs and satisfy their desires and protect their interests. Real love is best described as being unselfish in all aspects, even if a personal sacrifice is required in the relationship.

AUGUST 28

EVANGELIZE YOUR CHILDREN

He said to them, "Go into all the world and preach the good news to all creation. Whoever believes and is baptized will be saved."
Mark 16:15-16 NIV

My number one responsibility is to evangelize my children.

AUGUST 29

ROOM TO BREATHE

So then, just as you received Christ Jesus as Lord, continue to live in him, rooted and built up in him, strengthened in the faith as you were taught, and overflowing with thankfulness.
Colossians 2:6 NIV

I don't believe in harsh, inflexible discipline, even when it is well-intentioned. Children must be given room to breathe and grow and love.

AUGUST 30

INEVITABLE EXPRESSIONS

For all have sinned, and come short of the glory of God.
Romans 3:23 KJV

A child is naturally inclined toward rebellion, selfishness, dishonesty, aggression, exploitation, and greed. He does not have to be taught these behaviors. They are inevitable expressions of his humanness.

AUGUST 31

LOVE AND DISCIPLINE

For I have chosen him, so that he will direct his children and his household after him to keep the way of the LORD by doing what is right and just.
Genesis 18:19 NIV

Some young adults who have grown up in an atmosphere of love and discipline in balance are now raising their children that way.

SEPTEMBER

SEPTEMBER 1

GIVE YOURSELF WHOLLY

Be diligent in these matters; give yourself wholly to them, so that everyone may see your progress.
1 Timothy 4:15 NIV

This country's greatest need is for husbands to begin guiding their families, rather than pouring every physical and emotional resource into the mere acquisition of money.

SEPTEMBER 2

"ONE FLESH"

God "made them male and female." "For this reason a man will leave his father and mother and be united to his wife, and the two will become one flesh." So they are no longer two, but one.
Mark 10:6-8 NIV

Intimacy occurs when a man and woman, being separate and distinct individuals, are fused into a single unit that the Bible calls "one flesh." I'm convinced the human spirit craves this kind of unconditional love.

SEPTEMBER 3

THE CHOICE IS OURS

Neither height not depth, not anything else in all creation, will be able to separate us from the love of God that is in Christ Jesus our Lord.
Romans 8:35, 39 NIV

Hardship does not determine our behavior, but clearly it influences it. It requires courage to triumph over hardship despite unfavourable odds. The easier path is to wallow in self-pity – to freak out on drugs – to hate the world – to run – to withdraw – to compromise. Regardless of the ultimate course of action, however, the choice is ours alone.

SEPTEMBER 4

STOP YOUR ANGER!

Stop your anger! Turn off your wrath. Don't fret and worry - it only leads to harm.
Psalm 37:8 TLB

Screaming and accusing and berating are rarely successful in changing the behavior of human beings of any age.

SEPTEMBER 5

A LOVING RELATIONSHIP

A wife of noble character is her husband's crown, but a disgraceful wife is like decay in his bones.
Proverbs 12:4 NIV

There is nothing so ugly as a husband or wife who bitterly attacks and demeans his mate. But nothing is so beautiful as a loving relationship that conforms to God's magnificent design.

SEPTEMBER 6

COMMITMENT AS A FAMILY

Unless the Lord builds the house, its builders labor in vain.
Psalm 127:1 NIV

If a husband and wife are deeply committed to Jesus Christ, they enjoy enormous advantages over the family with no spiritual dimension.

SEPTEMBER 7

GOD HAS POURED OUT HIS LOVE

Hope does not disappoint us, because God has poured out his love into our hearts by the Holy Spirit, whom he has given us.
Romans 5:5 NIV

I see small children as vulnerable little creatures who need buckets of love and tenderness every day of their lives.

SEPTEMBER 8

A POSITIVE IMAGE

Blessed are they whose ways are blameless, who walk according to the law of the LORD. Blessed are they who keep his statutes and seek him with all their heart.
Psalm 119:1-2 NIV

If you let a child know that you think he is lazy, sloppy, untruthful, unpleasant, and thoughtless, he'll probably prove you are right. Obviously, it is much better to make him stretch to reach a positive image than stoop to match one at ground level.

SEPTEMBER 9

WHAT IS GOOD

He has showed you, O man, what is good. And what does the LORD require of you? To act justly and to love mercy and to walk humbly with your God.
Micah 6:8 NIV

The overcommitted lifestyle is the villain that destroys marriage, Christian devotion, emotional health, and the well-being of children. In my opinion, overwork is the sour note in the symphony of our values.

SEPTEMBER 10

THE NEED FOR PRAYER

*I want men everywhere to
lift up holy hands in prayer,
without anger or disputing.*
1 Timothy 2:8 NIV

It is impossible for me to overstate the need for prayer in the fabric of family life.

SEPTEMBER 11

SING OF THE LORD'S GREAT LOVE

I will sing of the LORD'S great love forever; with my mouth I will make your faithfulness known through all generations.
Psalm 89:1 NIV

The best source of guidance for parents can be found in the wisdom of the Judeo-Christian ethic, which orginated with the Creator and was then handed down generation by generation from the time of Christ.

SEPTEMBER 12

LIVE IN HARMONY

Live in harmony with one another.
Romans 12:16 NIV

The Christian way of life lends stability to marriage because its principles and values naturally produce harmony.

SEPTEMBER 13

WORK TO KEEP LOVE ALIVE

Above all, love each other deeply, because love covers a multitude of sins.
1 Peter 4:8 NIV

It is important to know that you have to work to keep love alive; you have to protect it and maintain it, just like you would a delicate flower.

SEPTEMBER 15

WHAT GOD HAS JOINED TOGETHER

Therefore what God has joined together, let man not separate.
Mark 10:9 NIV

Marriages that lack an iron-willed determination to hang together are like the unreinforced fragile bridges built two thousand years ago by the Romans. They appear to be secure and may indeed remain upright ... until they are put under heavy pressure.

SEPTEMBER 16

HAVING CONFIDENCE

The LORD seeth not as man seeth; for man looketh on the outward appearance, but the LORD looketh on the heart.
1 Samuel 16:7 KJV

Success breeds success. The best motivation for a slow learner is to know he is succeeding. If adults in his life show confidence in him, he will more likely have confidence in himself. We tend to act the way we think other people "see" us.

SEPTEMBER 17

A CHILD OF GOD

You are members of God's very own family, citizens of God's country, and you belong in God's household with every other Christian.
Ephesians 2:19 TLB

Is your child learning to accept himself as a child of God?

SEPTEMBER 18

SPIRIT-FOCUSED

Those who live according to the sinful nature have their minds set on what that nature desires; but those who live in accordance with the Spirit have their minds set on what the Spirit desires.
Romans 8:5 NIV

Parents can, and must, train, shape, punish, reward, teach, and love their kids during the formative years, to control that inner nature and keep it from tyrannizing the entire family. Ultimately, however, only Jesus Christ can make it "wholly acceptable" to the master.

SEPTEMBER 19

CONTROLLING IMPULSES

Our Fathers disciplined us for a little while as they thought best; but God disciplines us for our good, that we may share in his holiness.
Hebrews 12:10 NIV

Parents should introduce their child to discipline and self-control by the use of external influences when he is young. By being required to behave responsibly, he gains valuable experience in controlling his own impulses and resources.

SEPTEMBER 20

KEEP THE FAITH

*I have fought a good fight,
I have finished my course,
I have kept the faith.*
2 Timothy 4:7 KJV

Most of life is a marathon and not a sprint. It just goes on and on, and the pressure to give up seems to increase with the passage of time. That is certainly true of the Christian life.

SEPTEMBER 21

OBEY YOUR PARENTS

Children, obey your parents; this is the right thing to do because God has placed them in authority over you.
Ephesians 6:1 TLB

Two distinct messages must be conveyed to every child during his first forty-eight months: (1) "I love you more than you can possibly understand" and (2) "Because I love you I must teach you to obey me."

SEPTEMBER 22

LOVE OTHERS

"Love the Lord your God with all your heart and with all your soul and with all your strength and with all your mind," and, "Love your neighbor as yourself."
Luke 10:27 NIV

If we really love others as much as ourselves, we will give as much time and attention to helping them avoid pain and ridicule as we do ourselves.

SEPTEMBER 23

PUT OFF YOUR OLD SELF

You were taught, with regard to your former way of life, to put off your old self ... to be made new in the attitude of your minds; and to put on the new self, created to be like God in true righteousness and holiness.
Ephesians 4:22-24 NIV

Heredity does not equip a child with proper attitudes; children learn what they are taught. We cannot expect the coveted behavior to appear magically.

SEPTEMBER 24

NO BITTERNESS TAKES ROOT

Look after each other so that not one of you will fail to find God's best blessings. Watch out that no bitterness takes root among you, for as it springs up it causes deep trouble, hurting many in their spiritual lives.
Hebrews 12:15 TLB

Even genuine love between a man and woman is vulnerable to pain and trauma; it often wobbles when assaulted by life.

SEPTEMBER 25

THOROUGHLY EQUIPPED

All Scripture is God-breathed and is useful for teaching, rebuking, correcting and training in righteousness, so that the man of God may be thoroughly equipped for every good work.
2 Timothy 3:16 NIV

By a proper use of parental influence, we can provide our children with the inner strength necessary to survive the obstacles they will face. Perhaps we won't reconstruct the world, but we can help our children cope with it more successfully.

SEPTEMBER 26

THE PRIVILEGE OF BEING A CHILD

Children's children are a crown to the aged, and parents are the pride of their children.
Proverbs 17:6 NIV

Be patient and give your child time to mature. Work gently on the traits that concern you the most, but allow him the privilege of being a child. He will be one for such a brief moment, anyway.

SEPTEMBER 27

LOVE FOR GOD AND OUR NEIGHBOR

Beloved, let us love one another: for love is of God; and every one that loveth is born of God, and knoweth God. He that loveth not knoweth not God; for God is love.
1 John 4:7-8 KJV

The children of Christians need to learn empathy and kindness during the early years. After all, Jesus gave the highest priority to the expression of love for God and for our neighbor.

SEPTEMBER 28

SPIRITUAL COMMITMENT

*Remember your Creator
in the days of your youth.*
Ecclesiastes 12:1 NIV

We should lead our children into a deeply meaningful relationship with Jesus Christ early in life. The motivation and strength to live a life of purity is a by-product of this spiritual commitment and understanding.

SEPTEMBER 29

HONEST TESTIMONY

A truthful witness gives honest testimony, but a false witness tells lies. Reckless words pierce like a sword, but the tongue of the wise brings healing.
Proverbs 12:17-18 NIV

If we want to see honesty, truthfulness, and unselfishness in our offspring, then these characteristics should be the conscious objectives of our early instructional process.

SEPTEMBER 30

MAKE ALLOWANCE

Be patient with each other, making allowance for each other's faults because of your love.
Ephesians 4:2 TLB

A good marriage is not one where perfection reigns: it is a relationship where a healthy perspective overlooks a multitude of "unresolvables."

OCTOBER

OCTOBER 1

A SACRED BOND

Then the LORD God made a woman from the rib he had taken out of the man, and he brought her to the man ... For this reason a man will leave his father and mother and be united to his wife, and they will become one flesh.
Genesis 2:22, 24 NIV

The institution of marriage has been a sacred bond of fidelity between a man and a woman throughout history. The pledge of loyalty and mutual support represented by the marriage vows is a promise of commitment that extends to every aspect of life.

OCTOBER 2

DAILY ROUTINE

Surely goodness and mercy shall follow me all the days of my life.
Psalm 23:6 KJV

Children love daily routine activities of the simplest kind. You can turn the routine chores of living into times of warmth and closeness if you give a little thought to them.

OCTOBER 3

A STEADFAST MIND

You will keep in perfect peace him whose mind is steadfast, because he trusts in you. Trust in the LORD forever, for the LORD, the LORD, is the Rock eternal.
Isaiah 26:3 NIV

Most teenagers respect a guy or girl who has the courage to be his own person, even when being teased.

OCTOBER 4

KINDNESS

A kindhearted woman gains respect, but ruthless men gain only wealth. A kind man benefits himself; but a cruel man brings trouble on himself.
Proverbs 11:16-17 NIV

If it is desirable for children to be kind, appreciative, and pleasant, those qualities should be taught — not hoped for.

OCTOBER 5

THE WORK OF YOUR HAND

Yet, O LORD, you are our Father. We are the clay, you are the potter; we are all the work of your hand.
Isaiah 64:8 NIV

If jealousy is so common, then how can parents minimize the natural antagonism that children feel for their siblings? The first step is to avoid circumstances that compare them unfavorably with each other.

OCTOBER 6

GUARD YOUR AFFECTIONS

Guard your affections. For they influence everything else in your life.
Proverbs 4:13 TLB

The overwhelming feeling of being "in love" is not a very reliable emotion. The only way to know if you are in love with another person is to give yourselves plenty of time to get acquainted. Once marriage occurs, then your commitment to one another will be much more important than the feelings, which come and go.

OCTOBER 7

A PLAN FOR LIFE

I know whom I have believed, and am persuaded that he is able to keep that which I have committed unto him against that day.
2 Timothy 1:12 KJV

Each child can be made aware, beyond a shadow of a doubt, that he is a personal creation of God. He can know that the Creator has a plan for his life and that Jesus died for him.

OCTOBER 8

LOVE AND CONTROL

Let us not love with words or tongue but with actions and in truth.
1 John 3:18 NIV

Healthy parenthood can be boiled down to those two essential ingredients, love and control, operating in a system of checks and balances.

OCTOBER 9

ACCEPTANCE

Accept one another, then, just as Christ accepted you, in order to bring praise to God.
Romans 15:7 NIV

Children are incredibly vulnerable to rejection, ridicule, criticism, and anger at home, and they deserve to grow up in an environment of safety, acceptance, and warmth.

OCTOBER 10

SPIRITUAL WELFARE

But thanks be to God, who always leads us in triumphal procession in Christ and through us spreads everywhere the fragrance of the knowledge of him. For we are to God the aroma of Christ among those who are being saved and those who are perishing.
2 Corinthians 2:14-15 NIV

Our ultimate objective in living must be the spiritual welfare of our sons and daughters. If we lose it there, we have lost everything.

OCTOBER 11

A REFUGE

He who fears the LORD has a secure fortress, and for his children it will be a refuge.
Proverbs 14:26 NIV

There is a narrow difference between acceptable, healthy "awe" and destructive fear. A child should have a general apprehension about the consequences of defying his parents. By contrast, he should not lie awake at night worrying about parental harshness or hostility.

OCTOBER 12

BE AGREED

*Can two walk together,
except they be agreed?*
Amos 3:3 KJV

Don't marry someone with intolerable characteristics in the hope of changing him or her. If you can't live with someone who drinks, or someone who isn't a Christian, or someone who isn't clean, then don't marry that kind of person. The chances for miraculous improvements are slim. What you see is what you get!

OCTOBER 13

FEARS

I sought the LORD, and he answered me; he delivered me from all my fears.
Psalm 34:4 NIV

Anything that worries or troubles a child can result in school failure. For example, problems at home or feelings of inadequacy can prevent academic concentration.

OCTOBER 14

THE CONSCIENCE

Cling tightly to your faith in Christ and always keep your conscience clear, doing what you know is right. For some people have disobeyed their consciences and have deliberately done what they knew was wrong. It isn't surprising that soon they lost their faith in Christ after defying God like that.
1 Timothy 1:19 TLB

The proper programming of the conscience is one of the most difficult jobs associated with parenthood, and the one that requires the greatest wisdom.

OCTOBER 15

THE WIFE OF YOUR YOUTH

May you rejoice in the wife of your youth.
Proverbs 5:18 NIV

A woman finds life much more enjoyable if she knows she is the sweetheart, and not just the wife, of her husband.

OCTOBER 16

LOVING DISCIPLINE

Those whom I love I rebuke and discipline. So be earnest, and repent. ... I stand at the door and knock. If anyone hears my voice and opens the door, I will come in and eat with him, and he with me.
Revelation 3:19-20 NIV

When properly applied, loving discipline works! It stimulates tender affection, made possible by mutual respect between a parent and a child. It bridges the gap that otherwise separates family members who should love and trust each other.

OCTOBER 17

DIVINELY INSTITUTED

Then God blessed Noah and his sons, saying to them, "Be fruitful and increase in number and fill the earth."
Genesis 9:1 NIV

The family was divinely instituted and sanctioned in the beginning, when God created one man and one woman, brought them together, and commanded them to "be fruitful and multiply." The family is not merely human in origin. It is God's marvelous creation.

OCTOBER 18

INSTILLING OBEDIENCE

As servants of God we commend ourselves in every way: ... in purity, understanding, patience and kindness; in the Holy Spirit and in sincere love.
2 Corinthians 6:4, 6 NIV

You must keep a sense of humor during the twos and threes in order to preserve your own sanity. But you must also proceed with the task of instilling obedience and respect for authority.

OCTOBER 19

BIBLICAL CONCEPTS OF MORALITY

All have turned aside, they have together become corrupt; there is no one who does good, not even one.
Psalm 14:3 NIV

It is my belief that the weakening of the country's financial position and the difficulties its families and its children are experiencing can be traced to our departure from traditional values and Biblical concepts of morality.

OCTOBER 20

DIVORCE

"Why has God abandoned us?" you cry. I'll tell you why; it is because the Lord has seen your treachery in divorcing your wives who have been faithful to you through the years, the companions you promised to care for and keep ... The Lord, the God of Israel, says he hates divorce and cruel men. Therefore, control your passions – let there be no divorcing of your wives.
Malachi 2:14, 16 TLB

Divorce is not the answer to the problem of busy husbands and lonely wives.

OCTOBER 21

WORTH MORE

God knoweth your hearts: for that which is highly esteemed among men is abomination in the sight of God.
Luke 16:15 KJV

The Lord emphasizes in his Word that each of us is worth more than the possessions of the entire world. This is true just because we are human beings – not because of the way we look, or to whom we are married, or what our parents do, or how much money we have, or how much we have accomplished in life. Those earthly factors make no difference to God.

OCTOBER 22

THEY WILL FLOURISH

The righteous will flourish like a palm tree, they will grow like a cedar of Lebanon; planted in the house of the LORD, they will flourish in the courts of our God.
Psalm 92:12-13 NIV

Spiritual training should begin before children can even comprehend what it is all about. They should grow up seeing their parents on their knees before God, talking to him. They will learn quickly at that age and will never forget what they've seen and heard.

OCTOBER 23

RESPECT PARENTS

Honor your father and your mother, as the LORD your God has commanded you, so that you may live long and that it may go well with you in the land the LORD your God is giving you.
Deuteronomy 5:16 NIV

It is imperative that a child should be taught to respect his parents – not to satisfy their egos, but because his relationship with them provides the basis for his later attitude toward all other people.

OCTOBER 24

OUR REPUTATION

Live such good lives among the pagans that, though they accuse you of doing wrong, they may see your good deeds and glorify God.
1 Peter 2:12 NIV

Many children who fail in school are merely doing what they think others expect of them. Our reputation with our peers is indeed a very influential force in our lives.

OCTOBER 25

TO ASSIST PARENTS

Fix these words of mine in your hearts and minds. ... Teach them to your children, talking about them when you sit at home and when you walk along the road, when you lie down and when you get up.
Deuteronomy 11:18-19 NIV

Be careful whom you choose to trust with the body – and the soul – of your child. Educators, youth ministers, athletic coaches, music instructors, psychologists, counselors, and physicians are there to assist parents in raising their kids, not to replace them.

OCTOBER 26

FRUSTRATION

Hope deferred makes the heart sick; but when dreams come true at last, there is life and joy.
Proverbs 13:12 TLB

Is your child learning to tolerate minor frustration?

OCTOBER 27

GREED

*Greed causes fighting; trusting
God leads to prosperity.*
Proverbs 28:25 TLB

Never risk that which you cannot afford to lose.

OCTOBER 28

THE ART OF SELF-CONTROL

Like a city whose walls are broken down is a man who lacks self-control.
Proverbs 25:28 NIV

Children need to be taught self-discipline and responsible behaviour. They need assistance in learning how to handle the challenges and obligations of living. They must learn the art of self-control.

OCTOBER 29

THE GIVER OF LIFE

For God so loved the world, that he gave his only begotten Son, that whosoever believeth in him should not perish, but have everlasting life.
John 3:16 KJV

If I can lead but one lost human being to the personhood of Jesus Christ – the giver of life itself – then I need no other justification for my earthly existence.

OCTOBER 30

PEACE OF MIND AND HEART

I am leaving you with a gift – peace of mind and heart! And the peace I give isn't fragile like the peace the world gives. So don't be troubled or afraid.
John 14:27 TLB

Letting go is not an easy task, but good parenthood demands it.

OCTOBER 31

AN INNER MAINSTAY

If they fall it isn't fatal, for the Lord holds them with his hand.
Psalm 37:24 TLB

After age 13 to 16, some adolescents resent being told exactly what to believe; they do not want religion "forced down their throats," and they should be given more and more autonomy in what they believe. If the early exposure has been properly conducted, they will have an inner mainstay to steady them.

NOVEMBER

NOVEMBER 1

DEMONSTRATE APPRECIATION

The boundary lines have fallen for me in pleasant places; surely I have a delightful inheritance.
Psalm 16:6 NIV

Does your child see and hear you demonstrate appreciation to others in the family? to friends and acquaintances? to God?

NOVEMBER 2

LOSE YOUR LIFE FOR ME

For whoever wants to save his life will lose it, but whoever loses his life for me will save it.
Luke 9:24 NIV

Followers of the "me-first" philosophy have a very high ratio of suicide, divorce, and general neuroticism.

NOVEMBER 3

WILL HE NOT CLOTHE YOU?

See how the lilies of the field grow. They do not labor or spin. Yet I tell you that not even Solomon in all his splendor was dressed like one of these. If that is how God clothes the grass of the field ... will he not much more clothe you?
Matthew 6:28-30 NIV

Children of an appropriate age should be allowed to select their own clothes, within certain limits of the budget and good taste.

NOVEMBER 4

BE GENTLE

Let your gentleness be evident to all. The Lord is near.
Philippians 4:5 NIV

A child should not be punished for behavior that is not willfully defiant. When he forgets to feed the dog or make his bed or take out the trash – when he leaves your tennis racket outside in the rain or loses his bicycle – remember that these behaviors are typical of childhood. Be gentle as you teach him to do better.

NOVEMBER 5

RESPECT AND DIGNITY

It is by faith you stand firm.
2 Corinthians 1:24 NIV

I recommend a simple principle: when you are defiantly challenged, win decisively. When the child asks, "Who's in charge?" tell him. When he mutters, "Who loves me?" take him in your arms and surround him with affection. Treat him with respect and dignity, and expect the same from him.

NOVEMBER 6

CARE ABOUT PEOPLE

The King will reply, "I tell you the truth, whatever you did for one of the least of these brothers of mine, you did for me."
Matthew 25:40 NIV

One of the most important responsibilities in the Christian life is to care about other people — to smile at them and to be a friend of the friendless. God wants to use you to help his other children.

NOVEMBER 7

LET YOUR LIGHT SHINE

Neither do people light a lamp and put it under a bowl. Instead they put it on its stand, and it gives light to everyone in the house. In the same way, let your light shine before men, that they may see your good deeds and praise your Father in heaven.
Matthew 5:15-16 NIV

Take advantage of the opportunities that may be available in your local public school district to review textbooks that are being considered for adoption. Let the school board know of any anti-religious or immoral biases in the books.

NOVEMBER 8

WITH ALL YOUR HEART

Whatever you do, work at it with all your heart, as working for the Lord, not for men, since you know that you will receive an inheritance from the Lord as a reward.
Colossians 3:23-24 NIV

Children are terribly dependent on their parents, and the task of meeting their needs is a full-time job.

NOVEMBER 9

THEIR IDEAL

Be their ideal; let them follow the way you teach and live; be a pattern for them in your love, your faith, and your clean thoughts.
1 Timothy 4:12 TLB

Mothers and fathers are granted a single decade to lay a foundation of values and attitudes that will help their children cope with the future pressures and problems of adulthood.

NOVEMBER 10

BE HUMBLE AND GENTLE

Be completely humble and gentle; be patient, bearing with one another in love.
Ephesians 4:2 NIV

Parents who are cold and stern with their sons and daughters often leave them damaged for life. I don't believe in parental harshness.

NOVEMBER 11

SELF-SACRIFICE

The sacrifices of God are a broken spirit; a broken and contrite heart, O God, you will not despise.
Psalm 51:17 NIV

Since adult life requires sweat, self-sacrifice, and devotion to causes, school should help shape a child's capacity to handle this future responsibility.

NOVEMBER 12

SENSITIVITY

While he was still a long way off, his father saw him and was filled with compassion for him; he ran to his son, threw his arms around him and kissed him.
Luke 15:20 NIV

Sensitivity is the key word. It means "tuning in" to the thoughts and feelings of our kids, listening to the cues they give us and reacting appropriately to what we detect.

NOVEMBER 13

PERMISSIVENESS

Everyone who sins breaks the law; in fact, sin is lawlessness. But you know that he appeared so that he might take away our sins. And in him is no sin. No one who lives in him keeps on sinning.
1 John 3:4-6 NIV

Permissiveness has not simply failed as an approach to child rearing. It's been a disaster for those who have tried it.

NOVEMBER 14

FAMILIAR WITH ALL MY WAYS

O LORD, you have searched me and you know me. You know when I sit and when I rise; you perceive my thoughts from afar. You discern my going out and my lying down; you are familiar with all my ways.
Psalm 139:1-3

Did you know that God sees you when you hurt? He knows those deep fears and frustrations that you thought no one understood. He knows the longings of your heart.

NOVEMBER 15

PLAY IS IMPORTANT

Let them praise his name with dancing and make music to him with tambourine and harp. For the LORD takes delight in his people; he crowns the humble with salvation.
Psalm 149:3-4 NIV

Play is important in a child's life. Youngsters should not work all the time. The home and school should provide a healthy balance between discipline and play.

NOVEMBER 16

YOUR LAWS

I have chosen the way of truth; I have set my heart on your laws. I hold fast to your statutes, O LORD; do not let me be put to shame. I run in the path of your commands, for you have set my heart free.
Psalm 119:30-32 NIV

A child finds his greatest security in a structured environment where the rights of other people (and his own) are protected by definite boundaries.

NOVEMBER 17

A SOFT ANSWER

A soft answer turneth away wrath: but grievous words stir up anger.
Proverbs 15:1 KJV

Parents often use anger to get action instead of using action to get action. It is exhausting and it doesn't work! Trying to control children by screaming is as utterly futile as trying to steer a car by honking the horn.

NOVEMBER 18

YOUR WORDS

I have thought much about your words and stored them in my heart so that they would hold me back from sin.
Psalm 119:11 TLB

Is your child learning to memorize and quote Scripture?

NOVEMBER 19

A FATHER TO YOU

I will be a Father to you, and you will be my sons and daughters, says the Lord Almighty.
2 Corinthians 6:18 NIV

Young children typically identify their parents ... and especially their fathers ... with God.

NOVEMBER 20

THANK GOD

Every morning tell him, "Thank you for your kindness," and every evening rejoice in all his faithfulness.
Psalm 92:2 TLB

Is your child learning to thank God for the good things in life?

NOVEMBER 21

THE HEART OF THE CHILDREN

He shall turn the heart of the fathers to the children, and the heart of the children to their fathers.
Malachi 4:6 KJV

We must appeal again to him who promised in the concluding words of the Old Testament, "He will turn the hearts of the children to their fathers." That would be great news, indeed, for the families of the world.

NOVEMBER 22

TEACH THEM TO YOUR CHILDREN

Watch yourselves closely so that you do not forget the things your eyes have seen or let them slip from your heart as long as you live. Teach them to your children.
Deuteronomy 4:9 NIV

Parents should begin talking to their children at length while they are still babies. Interesting mobiles should be arranged around the crib. From then on through the toddler years, learning activities should be programmed regularly.

NOVEMBER 23

IN CONFIDENCE AND SECURITY

Blessed is the man who trusts in the LORD, whose confidence is in him. He will be like a tree planted by the water that sends out its roots by the stream.
Jeremiah 17:7-8 NIV

There are ways to teach a child of his genuine significance, regardless of the shape of his nose or the size of his ears or the efficiency of his mind. *Every* child is entitled to hold up his head, not in haughtiness and pride, but in confidence and security.

NOVEMBER 24

A SENSE OF APPRECIATION

Dirty stories, foul talk, and coarse jokes – these are not for you. Instead, remind each other of God's goodness, and be thankful.
Ephesians 5:4 TLB

Is your child already learning a sense of appreciation at this time of his life?

NOVEMBER 25

LET THE LITTLE CHILDREN COME TO ME

Jesus said, "Let the little children come to me, and do not hinder them, for the kingdom of heaven belongs to such as these."
Matthew 19:14 NIV

A toddler is the most hard-nosed opponent of law and order, and he honestly believes the universe circles around him. In his cute little way, he is curious and charming and funny and loveable and exciting ... and selfish and demanding and rebellious and destructive.

NOVEMBER 26

LEARNING IS IMPORTANT

And we, who with unveiled faces all reflect the Lord's glory, are being transformed into his likeness with ever-increasing glory, which comes from the Lord, who is the Spirit.
2 Corinthians 3:18 NIV

Learning is important because we are changed by what we learn, even if the facts are later forgotten. Learning changes values, attitudes, and concepts that don't fade in time.

NOVEMBER 27

HEALTHY SELF-CONCEPTS

He gave his laws to Israel and commanded our fathers to teach them to their children, so that they in turn could teach their children too.
Psalm 78:5-6 TLB

With few exceptions, our materialistic society is not going to reinforce healthy self-concepts in your children, and if these desirable attributes are to be constructed, only you can do it.

NOVEMBER 28

GOD'S BEHAVIOR

My thoughts are not your thoughts, neither are your ways my ways, saith the Lord.
Isaiah 55:8 KJV

There will often be times when God's behavior will be incomprehensible and confusing to us.

NOVEMBER 29

A SOLITARY SPARROW

I lie awake, lonely as a solitary sparrow on the roof.
Psalm 102:7 TLB

The three biggest sources of depression among women: (1) "I don't like myself." (2) "I have no meaningful relationship outside my home," and (3) "I am not even close to the man I love."

NOVEMBER 30

SENSITIVITY

Listen, my son, accept what I say, and the years of your life will be many. I guide you in the way of wisdom and lead you along straight paths.
Proverbs 4:10-11 NIV

Sensitivity to the feelings of the teen is paramount. If he or she wishes to talk, by all means, welcome the conversation. In other cases, parental guidance may be most effective if offered indirectly.

DECEMBER

DECEMBER 1

GENEROSITY

A farmer who plants a few seeds will get only a small crop, but if he plants much, he will reap much ... Yes, God will give you much so that you can give away much.
2 Corinthians 9:6, 11 TLB

How often does your child see you engaging in specific acts of generosity? Particularly, are you generous and unselfish in your relationships with others?

DECEMBER 2

RENEWING YOUR MIND

Do not conform any longer to the pattern of this world, but be transformed by the renewing of your mind.
Romans 12:2 NIV

The human brain is capable of storing two billion bits of data in a lifetime; education is the process of filling that memory bank with useful information and concepts. Most important, it should teach us how to think.

DECEMBER 3

EARN THE RIGHT TO LEAD

*Teach me your way, O LORD;
lead me in a straight path.*
Psalm 27:11 NIV

The ultimate paradox of childhood is that boys and girls want to be led by their parents, but they insist that their mothers and fathers earn the right to lead them.

DECEMBER 4

MADE PERFECT IN WEAKNESS

But he said to me, "My grace is sufficient for you, for my power is made perfect in weakness." Therefore I will boast all the more gladly about my weaknesses, so that Christ's power may rest on me.
2 Corinthians 12:9-10 NIV

The happiest people in the world are not those who have no problems, but the people who have learned to live with those things that are less than perfect.

DECEMBER 5

MAINTAIN HIS RESPECT

For God said, "Honor your father and mother."
Matthew 15:4 NIV

The most vital objective of disciplining a child is to gain and maintain his respect. If the parents fail in this task, life can become uncomfortable indeed.

DECEMBER 6

IMPORTANT TO THE HAPPINESS OF THE HOME

In vain you rise early and stay up late, toiling for food to eat.
Psalm 127:2 NIV

A mother should get our of the house completely for one day a week, doing something for sheer enjoyment. Even if it costs money for a baby-sitter, this kind of recreation is more important to the happiness of the home than buying new drapes or a power saw for Dad.

DECEMBER 7

OUR INIQUITIES

But we are all as an unclean thing, and all our righteousnesses are as filthy rags; and we all do fade as a leaf; and our iniquities, like the wind, have taken us away.
Isaiah 64:6 KJV

Suppose the parents of yesterday could visit our time to observe the conditions that prevail among our children. They would be appalled by the problems that have become widespread in our homes, schools, and neighborhoods.

DECEMBER 8

OVERPROTECTION

God sometimes uses sorrow in our lives to help us turn away from sin and seek eternal life. We should never regret his sending it.
2 Corinthians 7:10 TLB

Overprotection produces emotional cripples who often develop lasting characteristics of dependency and a kind of perpetual adolescence.

DECEMBER 9

INSULATION RATHER THAN ISOLATION

Let us not give up meeting together ... but let us encourage one another.
Hebrews 10:25 NIV

Most loneliness results from insulation rather than isolation. In other words, we are lonely because we insulate ourselves, not because others isolate us.

DECEMBER 10

BROTHERS LIVE IN UNITY

How good and pleasant it is when brothers live together in unity!
Psalm 133:1 NIV

Many of the emotional problems suffered of some adults can be traced to the viciousness and brutality of siblings and peers during their early home experiences.

DECEMBER 11

ONE IN SPIRIT

If you have any encouragement from being united with Christ ... then make my joy complete by ... having the same love, being one in spirit and purpose.
Philippians 2:1-2 NIV

The best way to get children to do what you want is to spend time with them before disciplinary problems occur – having fun together and enjoying mutual laughter and joy. When those moments of love and closeness happen, kids are not as tempted to challenge and test the limits.

DECEMBER 12

LEARN TO COPE

O God ... you have always cared for me in my distress; now hear me as I call again.
Psalm 4:1 TLB

Your child needs the minor setbacks and disappointments that come his way. How can he learn to cope with problems and frustration if his early experiences are totally without trial?

DECEMBER 13

OBEY AND SUBMIT

Obey your leaders and submit to their authority. They keep watch over you as men who must give an account.
Hebrews 13:17 NIV

Their respect for strength and courage makes children want to know how "tough" their leaders are. They will occasionally disobey parental instructions for the precise purpose of testing the determination of those in charge.

DECEMBER 14

HEALTHY SEXUAL ATTITUDES

You were bought at a price. Therefore honor God with your body.
1 Corinthians 6:20 NIV

The task of forming healthy sexual attitudes and understandings in children requires considerable skill and tact. For those parents who are able to handle the instructional process correctly, the responsibility should be retained in the home.

DECEMBER 15

THE GOD OF ALL COMFORT

Praise be to the God and Father of our Lord Jesus Christ ... who comforts us in all our troubles, so that we can comfort those in any trouble.
2 Corinthians 1:3-4 NIV

Every age poses its own unique threats to self-esteem. Little children typically suffer a severe loss of status during the tender years of childhood. Likewise, most adults are still attempting to cope with the inferiority experienced in earlier times.

DECEMBER 16

IT TAKES TIME

Mary sat on the floor, listening to Jesus as he talked. ... "There is really only one thing worth being concerned about. Mary has discovered it."
Luke 10:39, 42 TLB

Overcommitment and time pressure are the greatest destroyers of marriages and families. It takes time to develop any friendship ... whether with a loved one or with God himself.

DECEMBER 17

BE KIND TO OTHERS

Don't snap back at those who say unkind things about you. Instead, pray for God's help for them, for we are to be kind to others, and God will bless us for it.
1 Peter 3:9 TLB

The hostility in many marriages is a direct expression of deep hurt between husband and wife.

DECEMBER 18

THE BIBLICAL PRESCRIPTION FOR MARRIAGE

Seek ye first the kingdom of God, and his righteousness; and all these things shall be added unto you.
Matthew 6:33 KJV

There is still no substitute for the biblical prescription for marriage, nor will its wisdom ever be replaced.

DECEMBER 19

THE TONGUE OF THE WISE

Reckless words pierce like a sword, but the tongue of the wise brings healing.
Proverbs 12:18 NIV

The adolescent experience is typically characterized by emotional highs and lows, operating in cyclical fashion. If family members recognize the fluctuating personality pattern as normal, they might find it easier to live with the emotional, excitable, impressionable, erratic, idealistic romanticist known as an adolescent.

DECEMBER 20

EDIFYING EXPERIENCES

If you then, though you are evil, know how to give good gifts to your children, how much more will your Father in heaven give the Holy Spirit to those who ask him!
Luke 11:13 NIV

It is imperative that parents take the time and invest their resources in their children. The necessity for providing rich, edifying experiences for young children has never been so pressing as it is today.

DECEMBER 21

GOD'S LAWS

God's laws are perfect. They protect us, make us wise, and give us joy and light. God's laws are pure, eternal, just.
Psalm 19:7-9 TLB

God's laws will remain in force even if the entire world rejects them.

DECEMBER 22

EXCELLENT
MATERIALISM

He who loves money shall never have enough. The foolishness of thinking that wealth brings happiness!
Ecclesiastes 5:10 TLB

Excessive materialism in parents has the power to inflict enormous spiritual damage on our sons and daughters. If they see that we care more about things than people, if they recognize the hollowness of our Christian testimony, the result is often cynicism and disbelief.

DECEMBER 23

ROUTINE PANIC

Come, Lord, and show me your mercy, for I am helpless, overwhelmed, in deep distress; my problems go from bad to worse.
Psalm 25:16-17 TLB

Routine panic is becoming a way of life. Guess who is the inevitable loser from this breathless life-style? It's the little guy who is leaning against the wall with his hands in the pockets of his blue jeans.

DECEMBER 24

WORTHY OF ALLEGIANCE

Submit yourselves, then, to God. Resist the devil, and he will flee from you. Come near to God and he will come near to you.
James 4:7-8 NIV

Adult leadership is rarely accepted unchallenged by the next generation; it must be "tested" and found worthy of allegiance by the youngsters who are asked to yield and submit to its direction.

DECEMBER 25

THE BEAUTY OF JESUS' BIRTH AND DEATH

He came once for all ... to put away the power of sin forever by dying for us.
Hebrews 9:26 TLB

Is your child learning the beauty of Jesus' birth and death?

DECEMBER 26

PERSONAL AWARENESS

You are to give him the name Jesus, because he will save his people from their sins.
Matthew 1:21 NIV

There is no greater sense of self-esteem and personal worth than the personal awareness that comes from deeply ingrained spiritual values. Only Christ can provide the answers to questions such as: "Who am I?" "Who loves me?" "Where am I going?" and "What is the purpose of life?"

DECEMBER 27

PERMISSIVE ATTITUDES

Flee from sexual immorality. All other sins a man commits are outside his body, but he who sins sexually sins against his own body. Do you not know your body is a temple of the Holy Spirit?
1 Corinthians 6:18-19 NIV

It is impossible to shield youth from the permissive attitudes that are prevalent today. Television brings every aspect of sexual gratification into the sanctuary of one's living room.

DECEMBER 28

BE STRONG IN THE LORD

Finally, be strong in the Lord and in his mighty power.
Ephesians 6:10 NIV

There's no doubt about it: children are expensive little people. To raise them properly will require the very best that you can give of your time, effort, and financial resources.

DECEMBER 29

FAMILY RESOURCES

For riches can disappear as though they had the wings of a bird!
Proverbs 23:4-5 TLB

Allocate your family resources with the wisdom of Solomon. Don't spend more for a house or car than you can afford, leaving too few resources for dating, short trips, baby-sitters, etc.

DECEMBER 30

THE STANDARD

*If you obey him, all will
go well for you.*
Deuteronomy 6:18 TLB

God's Word is the standard for all human behavior and values.

DECEMBER 31

THE FRUIT OF RIGHTEOUSNESS

The fruit of righteousness will be peace; the effect of righteousness will be quietness and confidence forever.
Isaiah 32:17 NIV

Self-control, human kindness, respect, and peacefulness can again be manifest if we will dare to discipline in our homes and schools.